THE AMORINO GUIDE TO GELATO

© Hachette Livre (Le Chêne), Paris, 2013.
First published by Hachette Livre, Éditions du Chêne in France in 2013 as *Amorino, Trésors Glacés*.

First Skyhorse Publishing edition, 2020.

Translation © 2020 by Skyhorse Publishing, Inc.

Skyhorse Publishing books may be purchased in bulk at special discounts for sales promotion, corporate gifts, fund-raising, or educational purposes. Special editions can also be created to specifications. For details, contact the Special Sales Department, Skyhorse Publishing, 307 West 36th Street, 11th Floor, New York, NY 10018 or info@skyhorsepublishing.com.

Skyhorse® and Skyhorse Publishing® are registered trademarks of Skyhorse Publishing, Inc.®, a Delaware corporation. Visit our website at www.skyhorsepublishing.com.

10 9 8 7 6 5 4 3 2 1

Library of Congress Cataloging-in-Publication Data is available on file.

Cover design by Kai Texel

Print ISBN: 978-1-5107-5818-6
Ebook ISBN: 978-1-5107-6247-3

Printed in China

THE AMORINO GUIDE TO GELATO

Learn to Make Traditional Italian Frozen Desserts

Text
Stéphan Lagorce

Photography
Thomas Dhellemmes

Design
Cécile Coulier

Translation
Bob Mitchell

Skyhorse Publishing

PREFACE

To marry flavors with the smoothness of gelato, to harmonize the flavor of fruits with the coolness of sorbet: this is the passion of Amorino. Amorino exudes through its fundamental values the demand for quality as much as the culture of consistency and of taste. The tradition of artisanal gelato, at the heart of Italian culinary culture, is in harmony with the pleasure of producing flavors and garnishes.

Motivated every day by the desire to make excellent gelati as honestly as possible, it seemed obvious to us that we should share our passion, our expertise, and our recipes throughout this book. We are delighted to have you discover the magic of these frozen delicacies, an integral part of our native land.

May the authentically Italian frozen treats introduced to you in this book help you live a few cool, delicious moments of pure decadence. . .

Cristiano Sereni
& Paolo Benassi

TABLE OF CONTENTS

INTRODUCTION

The smoothness of gelato, the coolness of sorbet, the flavor of fruits, the bounty of flavors are those qualities that the lover of frozen treats seeks when he or she passes beyond the threshold of a frozen treat artisan's shop, facing the open storage containers of deliciousness right there in the glass case, just before making a choice and grabbing a cone.

Gelato is instantaneous delight, the taste's impulse, the openhearted punctuation mark after a meal, or the brief gastronomical break with which we gift ourselves simply for pleasure. These frozen creations can offer us endless combinations of flavors and an innumerable variety of desserts that we can make up thanks to them.

To celebrate one of the most beautiful treasures of Italian culinary traditions—to restore to it its standing as a homemade dish that endures—is altogether simple, despite a few stubborn conventional opinions. This is the promise made in the pages that follow.

From the making of traditional gelati (vanilla, chocolate, coffee, custard, yogurt) to the making of sorbets as close as possible to the fruit itself (strawberry, raspberry, lemon, mango), follow the advice and the secrets that we reveal to you to make your favorite frozen treats.

Don't have the time to run the ice cream maker to make a fabulous dessert? Learn to prepare and revisit some Italian pastry classics to accompany the frozen treats of the Amorino establishment: a dark chocolate affogato, a dish of tiramisu, a pistachio hot-and-cold, and more.

Allow yourself to be guided by your tastes and your taste buds. Frozen treats are gustatory joy epitomized . . .

INTRODUCTION TO FROZEN DESSERTS
- Equipment, Ingredients, Preservation Advice, Special Products -

The Pleasure of "Homemade"

Gelati, sorbets, ices, smoothies . . .
Frozen desserts, endlessly.

Gelati, sorbets, ices, smoothies: creations and frozen desserts are, contrary to conventional opinion, totally affordable when creating them yourself in your home. Often perceived as complex and delicate, these frozen specialties are, therefore, unjustly eliminated from the family culinary repertoire and quite often bought in stores. This reputation of being difficult is not really justified.

In this chapter, you're going to discover a large number of mostly commonsensical recommendations, tips, and advice, so you feel completely at ease with recipes that can, at first reading, seem difficult to master. Discover which equipment you should use and which ingredients to have in your pantry in order to prepare succulent gelati and tasty sorbets. Advice concerning preservation and storage is also offered so that you have all the help you need to pull off these frozen specialties, from the simplest to the most delicate.

EQUIPMENT

In the olden days, master artisans prepared their sorbets in barrels placed on ice extracted from snow-clad summits. The enlightened enthusiast of today finds at his or her disposal an abundant array of effective ice cream makers, well designed and more practical. Without them, it's impossible to make good gelati—rich and smooth. Other equipment will be equally useful to you to create your frozen treats.

Mixing
Hand whisk
Wooden or plastic spoon
Bowls and mixing bowls

Cooking
Saucepan
Frying pan
Electric oven and baking sheet
Parchment paper

Straining
Conical strainer, fine strainer, or sieve

Stocking
Storage containers for gelati and sorbets
Airtight containers (for syrups, gelati that are chilling, sauces, coulis . . .)

Preparing and Presenting
Whipping siphon (for mousses and whipped creams)
Silicon molds (to form gelato)

Measuring
Electric scale (precise to the ounce)
Thermometer (for cooking sugar, meringues, sauces)
Measuring glass (precise to the fluid ounce)

Mixing and texturing
Electric beater (for meringues, zabagliones, mousse, whipped cream . . .)
Mixer (at least 1-quart capacity and working at 1,500 turns/minute minimum)

Churning
Plug-in ice cream makers
When connected to the power supply, these models have their own cooling unit. They are the best appliances for making gelato, since they function until the gelato or sorbet is fully ready. They are available in various sizes, designs, and programming. Choose the least complex ones (sometimes the most reliable) with a serviceable volume of 1 to 2 quarts, which is sufficient for household use.

Battery-run ice cream makers
When in use, the battery delivers "heat extractions" (coldness) to the ingredients while you prepare your frozen treats. When the battery has delivered all its "heat extractions," your preparation can no longer congeal. These models may be suitable, but each time, you will have to begin your gelato and sorbet preps when they are already quite cold; otherwise, the gelato or sorbet will remain hopelessly liquid.

PRESERVATION

The preservation of frozen ingredients is a fundamental principle, imperative to the flavor of gelati and to dietary hygiene. Above all, do not neglect this aspect of the process.

Gelati and sorbets

At home, gelati and sorbets should be stored in freezers programmed to reach a temperature of 0°F. At this temperature, the various components of the gelati and sorbets become (almost) inert: the bacteria can no longer develop, and the phenomena of oxidation and staling are slowed quite a bit. Thus, in essence, a gelato, or a sorbet, can keep for up to 18 months, without any damage to its constitution. As far as taste is concerned, that's a different story. With time, the frozen ice crystals end up developing, connecting, growing, and, little by little, forming an unpleasant consistency. The very velvety texture homemade gelati and sorbets have when they are first removed from the ice cream maker hardens after barely a few days. To prevent this from happening, you will find at the end of each recipe a tip to avoid this mishap. Likewise, refer to p. 26, which returns in greater detail regarding this topic.

A few practical precautions

At regular intervals, check the "true" temperature of your freezer with a thermometer. When you stock your gelati and sorbets, place them in clean and well-dried food containers. Always cover them with a thin covering when you stock them to prevent them from being saturated with the flavors of other nearby products (garlic, fish, meat . . .). Date clearly every product that you freeze and don't keep them for more than 4 to 5 months.

Sauces and side dishes

By definition, these products (aside from caramelized nuts) are a lot more fragile than others, since they are not frozen. Fruit coulis, for instance, don't run major risks, but sauces containing eggs are themselves extremely sensitive products.

A few practical precautions

When you cook a sauce with eggs, check its cooking temperature: 185°F suffices to pasteurize it. Have these sauces cool quickly. Place them in the fridge in an airtight container as soon as they are chilling. Consume them quickly, within two days after they are cooked.

GELATO INGREDIENTS

No good gelato exists without good ingredients! This mantra is the best guarantee of high-quality gelato and frozen desserts. Fortunately, good ingredients are easy to find, since most of them (with few exceptions) are the products of everyday consumption.

Dairy products

Milk
Half-and-half or fresh whole milk is ideal for giving body and taste to your preparations. As for powdered milk, choose a nonfat milk.

Butter
Orient your preference toward soft butter or, better yet, "extrafine" (made from pasteurized cream), whose inimitable flavor works wonders in gelati.

Cream
Choose light cream sold in the chilled food aisle (and not UHT light cream with a long shelf life). For thick crème fraîche, when a recipe requires it, choose the best quality, preferably organic with a seal of approval.

Mascarpone cream
Lean toward an Italian brand of mascarpone sold in a container, with a seal of approval if possible.

Yogurt
If you don't prepare your yogurt yourself, choose yogurts made with whole milk and produced by a reputable brand.

Eggs
As much as possible, prepare your gelati only with organic or extra fresh eggs. Look at the package for organic (hens raised on organic feed and with access to the outdoors) or cage-free (non-organic hens with access to open areas).

Honey
Choose very strong-tasting and fragrant honeys (*mille-fleurs*, lavender . . .), whether liquid or solid. If you choose a honey that is too bland, your gelato will only taste like sugar.

Chocolate
Favor native chocolates that evolve from extremely distinctive flavors. Try to choose good grocery products in order to get away from generic and uninteresting tastes. Rather, lean toward dark chocolate containing at least 65 percent cacao.

Cocoa

Natural cocoa powder is now available in stores. Trickier to find but nearly irreplaceable, cocoa paste will let you make perfect gelati. You can replace it with chocolate that is 99 percent cacao.

Praline

A mixture (in equal parts) of roasted hazelnuts and finely ground sugar, this fragrant paste lets you prepare delicious hazelnut gelato. You will find it on the Internet and in a few gourmet shops that specialize in kitchen goods and products.

Vanilla

For your gelati and desserts, make yourself happy with the best and choose gorgeous bourbon vanilla beans, certainly rather costly, but so fragrant. Avoid extracts and other flavorings.

Coconut

Choose UHT coconut milk in cartons or the highest quality powder (of known origin and whose flavors are listed).

Coffee

As with chocolate, lean toward native coffees that evolve from assertive and distinctive characteristics. You can buy them ground. There are also liquid coffee extracts, which are quite practical to use and produce great results.

Nuts

Whether they are roasted or not, walnuts, hazelnuts, almonds, pistachios, etc., always bring an inimitable flavor, as long as they are top quality. Lean toward products whose source and quality you know and which are preferably packaged in containers with an inert gas that prevents them from going bad.

Spice cookies

For spice cookie gelato, there are three possible solutions: make them based on your own cookie recipe; buy the cookies that you like, then crush them; or buy cookie dough in the store (which perfectly suits the recipe proposed on p. 78).

Other products

Alcohol

If you wish to add alcohol to your gelati, once again, only choose the best and use in moderation. Amaretto, citrus liqueurs, cognac, and Armagnac will all bring an inimitable stylishness to your recipes.

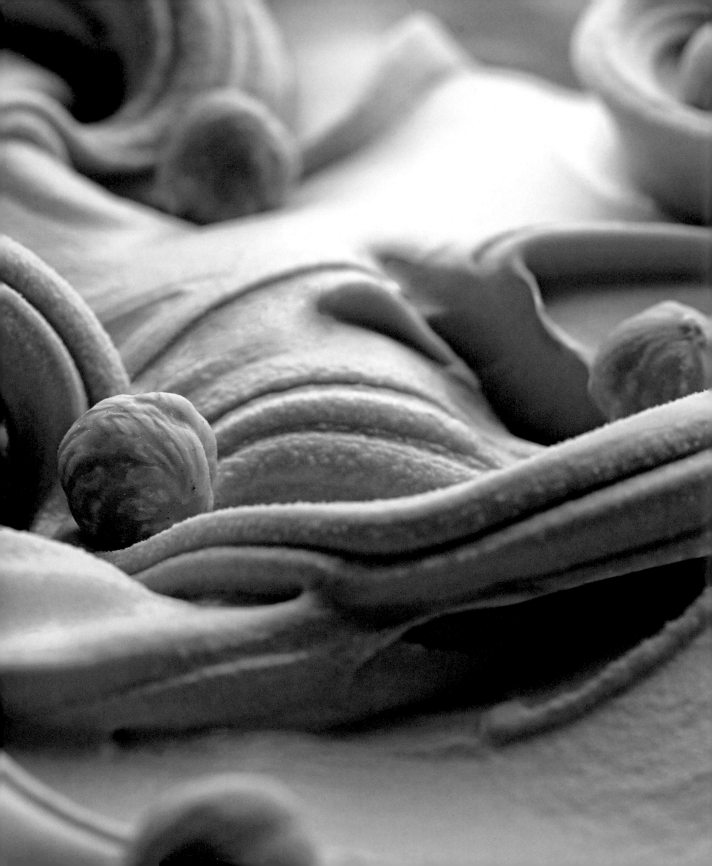

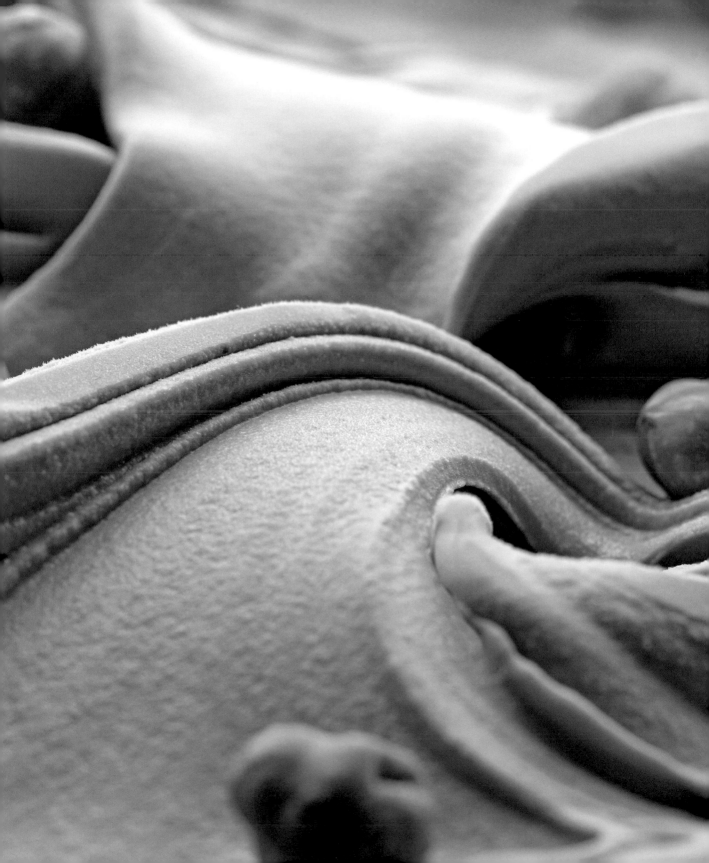

INGREDIENTS FOR SORBETS

*Making sorbets is very simple; in short, they contain
fruits, sugar, and water. The quality of the fruits ultimately determines
the success of the result. Knowing how to prepare a delicious sorbet
consists, to a great extent, in knowing how to buy good fruit at the right moment.*

Red berries

Strawberries, raspberries, black currants, red currants, gooseberries, cherries, figs . . . Buy products in containers which allow you to verify their quality: firm texture, beautiful colors, penetrating flavor. If you can't find good fresh red berries, fall back on frozen fruits (preferably organic) that are, usually, of good quality. Thaw them, transform them into sorbets (p. 83) or coulis and sauces (p. 197), then consume them at once.

Yellow fruits

Peaches, nectarines, apricots, melons, plums, pears . . . Their respective seasons are short, so don't miss them, because these are the only times of the year when you'll be able to buy them at their peak for yourself. Give in to fresh peach sorbet in the fall and fresh pear sorbet in the summer! Yet remember that you'll be able to use these products in the form of purées that are uncooked (p. 35) or cooked (p. 34: "cooked fruits").

Exotic fruits

Pineapples, mangoes, guavas, lychees, bananas . . . Ideally, look for them in season (better at year's end) and in Asian grocery stores, where, being very popular, the inventory rotates regularly. Try pink guavas, mini bananas, Indian Alphonso mangoes, and Victoria pineapples in sorbets, which can produce so many unforgettable delights (see the sorbet recipes, pp. 83 to 107).

Water

When water has to be incorporated into a sorbet, always pick a mineral water or a spring water, as neutral as possible, and not tap water (unless you first boil it for a minute, to get rid of the undesirable flavors that could alter the taste that you are trying to achieve).

Sugar

For sorbets, you use a prepared syrup (p. 32). The goal is for this syrup to be as neutral in taste as possible so that the flavor of the fruits alone is made prominent. To prepare it, choose a white powdered sugar—a classic.

SPECIAL INGREDIENTS
FOR GELATI AND SORBETS

---

*A good gelato is only prepared with natural ingredients,
from the best source, of the greatest freshness, and (if possible) a product of
organic agriculture. In order to give your gelato a velvety, unmatched texture while
reducing the quantity of fat it contains (notably, crème fraîche), you should incorporate
"special" ingredients that are easy to find and from a natural source.*

In the recipes included on the following pages, these ingredients are mentioned in the *"For an even smoother, more velvety gelato"* paragraph. You can choose to use them or not: your gelati will be delicious, no matter what. Just know that gelati prepared without these "special" ingredients seem to be less delicate and less smooth in your mouth, and, if you keep them in the freezer, harden quite solidly. Therefore, you should consider taking them out for a little while at room temperature before eating them. You will find these ingredients in kitchen supply stores and at online shops.

Glucose powder
Its taste is a lot less "sugary" than that of its cousin, sucrose (powdered sugar). It prevents the formation of large crystals in gelato. You can find it in kitchen supply stores and at online shops.

Dextrose
This sugar, common in the food industry, has the appearance of a fine white powder reminiscent of powdered sugar. Melting during the preparation at the time of cooking, it "fixes" the water (contained in the milk) and allows for a perfect distribution of the ingredients.

Maltodextrin
Despite its barbarous name, it's only one sugar among many. This white, fine powder—which is not very sweet to the taste—concentrates the gelato to give it a perfect texture, even after a few hours in the freezer.

Guar and carob
These natural, slightly beige legumes are food additives by simply grinding the seeds of the guar and carob trees. They thicken the gelato, even in very small amounts (most often 0.2 percent); they enrich it without requiring the addition of great quantities of butter or cream, making it easy to digest and pleasant.

Lecithin
This ingredient is found in its natural state in numerous foods like eggs and soy. This slightly beige fatty substance is a natural emulsifier that allows the fats in the gelato to bond with the water contained in the milk during the solidifying stage. So, the gelato always seems smooth and rich to the taste.

INTERMEDIATE PREPARATIONS
FOR GELATO

---

*While the process of making sorbets is to prepare a fruit purée, sweeten it,
and churn it, that of making gelato is quite different. In effect, the basis of the preparation
is milk. You must be able to properly add flavor to it in order to make an excellent gelato.*

To flavor gelato, you use the ancient principle of infusion: the flavors travel from the most concentrated ingredient (vanilla, tea, cinnamon . . .) to the least (milk). However, to get the expected results, you must follow a few rules:

• Never boil the infusion (then it would diminish the flavor);
• Break up the ingredient that gives the taste to the milk (so that it releases more flavoring);
• Respect the infusion time of the ingredients (very short for tea, long for liquid);
• Be sure to cover the container during the infusion (to limit the loss of flavoring);
• Prepare the infusions in saucepans made of stainless steel (to avoid the metallic taste).

Vanilla infusion
Fold the bean in two, then collect the black seeds with the point of your knife. Add the half-beans and seeds to the cold milk. Heat while combining, then, as soon as the milk simmers, remove it from the heat. Cover, let cool, then filter and prepare the gelato following the recipe.

Tea infusion
Infusing the tea for too long releases some very bitter compounds. So you must extract the flavorings but not the undesirable tastes. Heat the milk added to the cream (or water if it's a sorbet) until it reaches the correct temperature. Add the tea and cover. Let it steep away from the heat, then strain at the recommended time. Let it cool and prepare the gelato or the sorbet. For black tea, let it infuse 6 to 7 minutes at 195°F; for jasmine tea, let it infuse 3 to 4 minutes at 175°F; for Matcha tea, combine in liquid at 195°F.

Flower infusion (lavender, orange blossom . . .)
Likewise, lengthy infusion times release bitter tastes. Combine the milk and the tea with the flowers, heat to a temperature of 185 to 195°F. Cover and allow to infuse for about ten minutes. Filter, then let cool before preparing the gelato.

INTERMEDIATE PREPARATIONS
FOR SORBETS

To save some time and to facilitate the technique: these are the two equally important goals that the accomplished professional, as much as the amateur frozen dessert maker, must keep in mind. Reduce the work you need to do by preparing various components of the gelato in advance and set aside intentionally.

To prepare sorbets, one often uses syrups. You will find recipes and the correct proportions to prepare them yourself, then you will just need to blend them with the other ingredients and strain them into an ice cream maker. That will allow you to make an excellent sorbet in less than 5 minutes!

SUGAR SYRUP

Commonly used for the preparation of sorbets, sugar syrup mixes easily with fruit pulps and thus avoids the lengthy mixing times needed when using other forms of sugar. It's easy to make and keep for a long time. You can prepare it with different kinds of sugar: powdered, granulated, white, brown, cane, etc. When you prepare the sugar syrup, you can add herbs, spices, and aromatics to it, which, by infusion, flavor it pleasantly (e.g. sugar syrup and mint, which nicely suits strawberry mint sorbet). This syrup will be useful to you for sorbet recipes (p. 83). You can also use it to sweeten fruit coulis (p. 210) and to cook fruits with syrup (p. 34).

Sugar syrup
2.2 lbs sugar
1 quart water

1. In a saucepan, add the sugar and water. Heat on a high flame, stirring often with a hand whisk. As soon as the syrup starts to boil, remove the pan from the heat and let cool.
2. If you prepare it in advance, pour the cold syrup into a glass bottle, close it, and keep the syrup in a cool place.

Mint syrup
Prepare the recipe as listed above, adding 20 mint leaves at the same time as the sugar and the water. Let the leaves infuse in the syrup until thoroughly cooled, then filter the syrup. If you prepare it in advance, pour it in a bottle and keep it in a cool place.

Ginger syrup
Prepare the recipe as listed above, adding ¼ cup of peeled fresh ginger cut in fine slices, at the same time as the sugar and water. Allow the slices to infuse in the syrup until thoroughly cooled, then filter the syrup.

COOKED FRUITS

Cooked in a light syrup, seasonal fruits take on a creamy texture perfectly in keeping with your frozen treat preparations. The flesh of the fruits becomes tender, and the heat reveals or creates new flavors. What's more, the cooking stabilizes the fruits, solidifies their color, and allows you ultimately to make desserts of almost professional quality!

Amarena (sour) cherries in syrup
4½ lbs sugar
1 quart water
3⅓ lbs cherries (Morellos, if possible)

1. In a saucepan, add 2 lbs of the sugar and the water. Bring to a boil, then keep warm on a low flame.
2. Remove the cherry stems, then pit them gently without bruising them too much.
3. Immerse the cherries in the hot syrup, let simmer at medium heat for about 15 minutes (more or less depending on the age of the fruits).
4. Drain the cherries and put them aside. Add the rest of the sugar to the syrup. Bring to a boil, skim, then immerse the cherries in the warm syrup. Let cool completely.

Preservation
This preparation keeps for 2 to 3 weeks in the fridge.

Use
Top your gelato and sorbet cups with the cherries and, especially, with their syrup flavored from the cooking. You can also blend the fruit with the cooking syrup and incorporate this coulis into the fior di latte gelato (p. 68), at the end of the mixing process. Also consider incorporating whole or chopped Amarena cherries into your gelato (vanilla, custard . . .).

Pears (and other fruits) in syrup
4½ lbs sugar
2 quarts water
1 vanilla bean
4½ lbs pears
1 lemon

1. In a saucepan, add the sugar, water, and vanilla bean cut in two lengthwise. Bring to a boil, then keep warm on a low flame.
2. Peel the pears, hollow them out with an apple corer, cut them in two lengthwise. Cut the lemon in two and rub the pear halves with the lemon.
3. Immerse the pears in the hot syrup, let simmer at medium heat for about 20 minutes (more or less, depending on the age of the fruits).
4. Remove the pan from the heat, place the pears in jars, cover with hot syrup, close the jars, let cool.

Preservation
This preparation keeps for 2 to 3 weeks in the fridge.

Use
Use the cooked pears when they are cold. Combine them gently in their syrup to prepare coulis. Whole or sliced, they accompany gelato and sorbets equally nicely.

Option
Replace the syrup water with red wine and the vanilla with cinnamon.

Other possible fruits
Yellow and white peaches, plums, pineapples, mangoes, figs (very short cooking time), nectarines, apricots: prepare them the same way after having peeled them and, if necessary, pitted them.

FRUIT PURÉES

Neither good sorbets nor good coulis without good fruit purées! These very important foundations you must know how to make are quite easy to prepare, providing that you own a mixer and, in certain cases, a sieve or a fine strainer. They are, however, quite fragile: their flavor, their texture, their color change very rapidly, since you prepare them with raw fruits. Therefore, you must use them or preserve them by freezing as soon as they are ready.

Red berry purées
4½ lbs fruits (strawberries, raspberries, black currants, individually or combined)
1 lemon

1. Prepare the fruits: depending on the fruit, remove the stems, sort them, or wash them (never wash raspberries, for instance).
2. Squeeze the juice from the lemon.
3. Gently combine the fruits with the lemon juice. Filter the resulting pulp in a conical strainer (or a fine strainer or a sieve) to eliminate the seeds or achenes. Use the remaining purée for your sorbets, coulis, or gelato immediately.

Preservation
Placed in a hermetically sealed container, this purée keeps for 3 days in the fridge and 6 months in the freezer.

Yellow fruit purées
4½ lbs fruits (peaches, apricots, nectarines, mangoes, pineapples, guavas . . .)

1 lemon
1 orange
½ cup very cold mineral water

1. Prepare the fruits: depending on the fruit, remove the stems, peel them, remove the pits, sort them, or wash them.
2. Squeeze the juice from the lemon and the orange.
3. Gently combine the fruits with the citrus juice and water. Filter the resulting pulp in a conical strainer (or a fine strainer or a sieve). Immediately use the purée for your sorbets, coulis, or gelato.

Preservation
Placed in a hermetically sealed container, this purée keeps for 3 days in the fridge and 6 months in the freezer.

Purées made from zests
Always choose organic fruits. Only use the colored part of the peel (the rest being quite bitter). Chop it coarsely, then add it to the cold milk or fruit juice. Heat, while combining, then, as soon as the liquid is hot, remove the pan from the heat. Cover, let cool, then filter and prepare the gelato or the sorbet, depending on the recipe.

Preservation
Placed in a hermetically sealed container, this purée keeps for 3 days in the fridge and 6 months in the freezer.

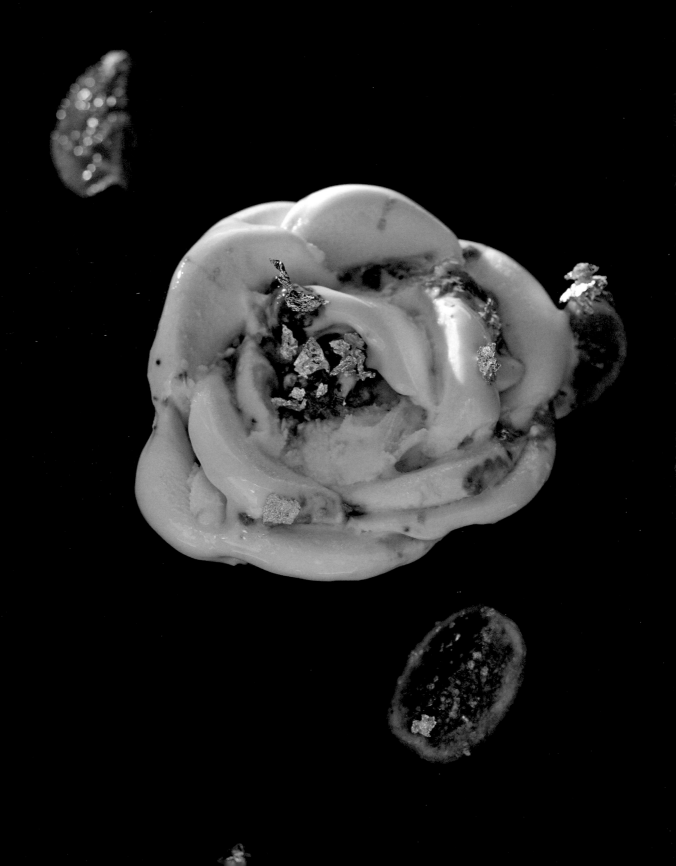

GELATO RECIPES
- Chocolate, Amarena (sour cherries), fior di latte, vanilla, coffee -

Italian gelato,
a tradition plain and simple

In Italy, gelato is an institution. You only have to walk through the streets of Rome, Milan, or Naples to see that the gelato artisans there are really numerous and, from the simplest to the most sophisticated, their gelati make everyone happy.

How do we recognize a "real" authentic Italian gelato? It is of course by its always unmistakable flavor and its unmatched smoothness. The texture of Italian gelato is in fact unique in its genre. It is never hard; it is never firm; it is never brittle. This distinct consistency is of course due to the recipe, which must be well balanced. It's especially important to the "freshness" of the gelato that one consumes it as soon as it is ready, or very soon after . . . It is precisely when it is removed from from the mixer that it must be tasted—still supple, creamy, and so smooth. In fact—and this is another secret of the Italian tradition—the gelati are consumed at a temperature between approximately 14 and 18°F, and not at 0°F and even still colder, as we have stated elsewhere!

As for ingredients, to be satisfied you must have the best, quite simply! No good gelato is without good milk, good cream, quality eggs, and flavorful ingredients. In this regard, it is important, even necessary, to be really demanding and discerning with what ingredients you choose to incorporate in your recipes.

Finally, another detail of gelati, in Italy: they like to garnish them in the storage containers where they store them. Powdered bitter cocoa, cookies, liqueurs, nuts, cooked and candied fruits: the imagination is the sole limit to the possible arrangements and embellishments. It's up to you to invent your own!

YOGURT GELATO

This gelato, very light and tart, always surprises and delights. The quality of the yogurt is what determines the quality of the gelato. Buy high-quality fermented yogurts, or better yet, prepare them yourself. For a change, you can also make this gelato with a nice whipped fromage blanc.

Difficulty: easy
Serves: about 6 people
Preparation time: 15 minutes
Cooking time: 2 to 3 minutes
Chill time: 5 to 6 hours
In ice cream maker: about 40 minutes

INGREDIENTS:
1½ cups whole milk
⅛ cup powdered milk
1 cup powdered sugar
1½ cups plain unsweetened
  yogurt

1. In a mixer, add the cold milk, powdered milk, and sugar. Mix for a few moments. If you don't own a mixer, combine these ingredients in a mixing bowl with a hand whisk.

2. Pour this mixture into a saucepan. Heat, stirring constantly with a whisk. When the contents just begin to simmer (at a temperature of 185°F), remove the pan from the heat and let cool thoroughly. Add the yogurt.

3. Place the ingredients in a hermetically sealed container and, if possible, let it cool in the fridge for 5 or 6 hours.

4. Just under an hour before serving the dessert, pour the contents into an ice cream maker and let it set. When the gelato is set, eat it right away. If you're not ready to eat it, cover it with plastic wrap and store it in the freezer until ready to eat.

Gorgeous . . . and good, too!
With this gelato, play with the lightness and the freshness to the fullest! Serve it with fresh fruit: raspberries, strawberries, quartered peaches; a hint of chopped mint and, possibly, a little strawberry coulis (p. 210) or a few crystallized lemon peels.

For an even smoother, more velvety gelato
Add the following ingredients, combining them with half of the cold milk: ⅛ cup dextrose, ⅛ cup maltodextrin, ¼ tsp guar flour, ½ tsp soy lecithin, and ¹⁄₁₆ cup glucose powder. Integrate this mixed milk at the start of step 2. The ingredients here are natural. They come from seeds or are very simple sugars. You can very easily find them either on the Internet or in shops marketing kitchen goods and products. See p. 26 for more information.

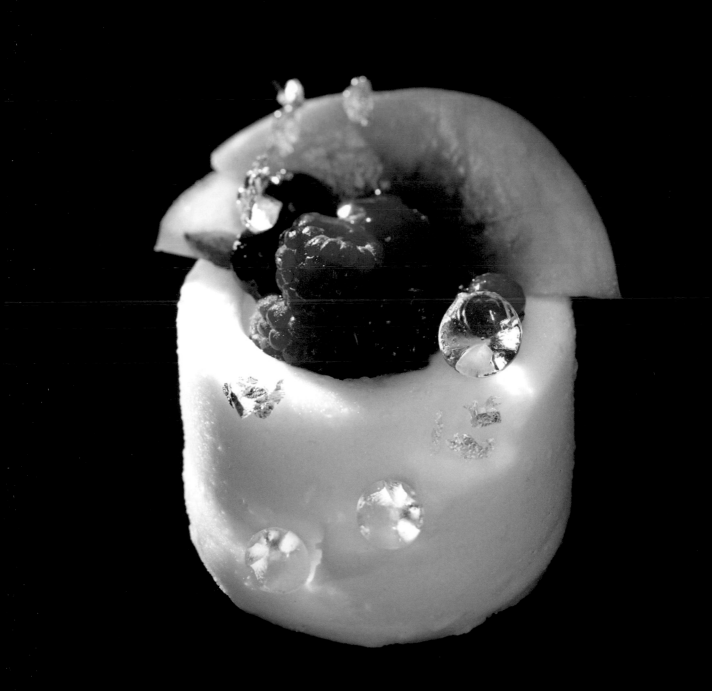

FIG MASCARPONE GELATO

The smoothness of mascarpone and the sensuous flavor of the figs make this gelato a true must-have—to prepare in the fall, of course. You can also add some caramelized nuts to create a more complex flavor.

Difficulty: easy
Serves: about 6 people
Preparation time: 20 minutes
Cooking time: 2 to 3 minutes
Chill time: 6 to 7 hours
In ice cream maker: about 40 minutes

INGREDIENTS:
6 oz of fresh figs
1 pat butter
4 tbsp brown sugar
2 cups milk
½ cup light cream
⅛ cup powdered milk
1 cup powdered sugar
1 cup mascarpone

1. Rinse the figs, cut them in quarters. In a frying pan, melt the butter until it foams. Add the figs and the brown sugar. Pan-fry a few minutes (no more), letting the sugar caramelize. Remove from the heat and let cool. Cut the fruits coarsely, place them in the freezer, at least 1 hour before beginning the gelato.

2. In a mixer, add the cold milk, light cream, powdered milk, and sugar. Mix for a few moments. If you don't own a mixer, whisk these ingredients by hand in a mixing bowl.

3. Pour the contents into a saucepan. Heat, stirring constantly with a whisk. When the contents just begin to simmer (at 185°F), remove the pan from the heat and let cool thoroughly. Then add the mascarpone.

4. Place the contents in a hermetically sealed container and let it cool in the fridge for 5 to 6 hours.

5. One hour before dessert time, pour the contents in the ice cream maker and let it set. When the gelato is set, add the fig pieces and their cooking juices; don't combine too much. Place it in a storage container and eat right away, or cover it with plastic wrap and store it in the freezer until ready to serve.

Gorgeous . . . and good, too!
Serve this gelato in sundae dishes with fresh quartered figs. Top with a few *contucci* (biscotti) fragments.

For an even smoother, more velvety gelato
Add the following ingredients (p. 26), combining them with half of the cold milk: ⅛ cup dextrose, ⅛ cup maltodextrin, ¼ tsp guar flour, ½ tsp soy lecithin, ¹⁄₁₆ cup glucose powder. Integrate this mixed milk with the rest of the ingredients at the start of step 2. The ingredients here are natural. They come from seeds or are very simple sugars. You can very easily find them either on the Internet or in shops marketing kitchen goods and products.

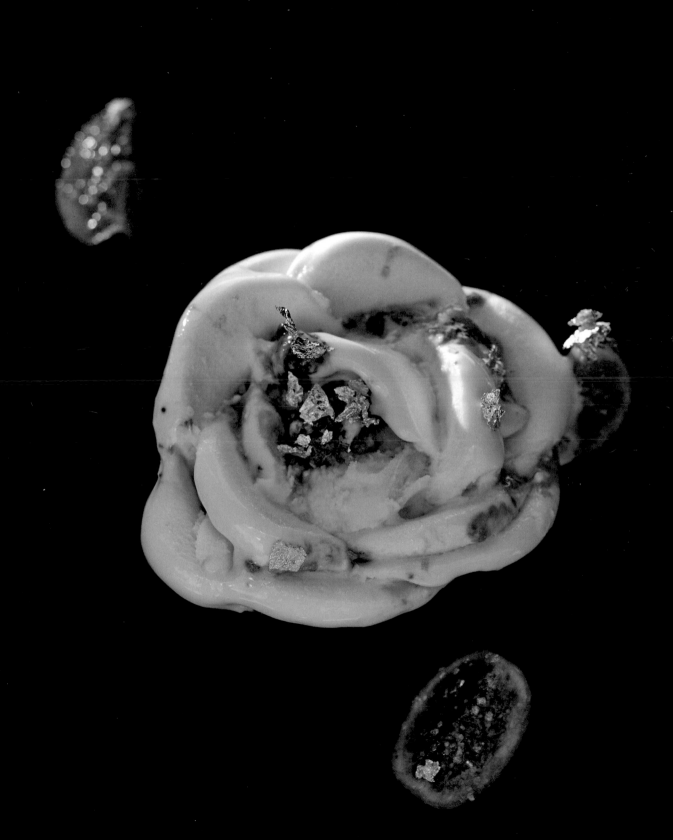

TIRAMISU GELATO

Transforming this great classic into gelato is a food-lover's joy that's irresistible to everyone! Serve this gelato as soon as it's done. Smooth, almost creamy, is how experienced gourmets appreciate it.

Difficulty: easy
Serves: about 6 people
Preparation time: 15 minutes.
Cooking time: 2 to 3 minutes
Chill time: 5 to 6 hours
In ice cream maker: about 40 minutes

INGREDIENTS
2½ cups milk
¼ cup light cream
1 egg yolk
⅛ cup powdered milk
1/16 cup coffee extract (or 1 level
   teaspoon freeze-dried coffee)
1 cup powdered sugar
½ cup mascarpone

1. In a mixer, add the cold milk, light cream, egg yolk, powdered milk, coffee, and sugar. Mix for a few moments. If you don't own a mixer, whisk these ingredients by hand in a mixing bowl.

2. Pour the contents into a saucepan. Heat, stirring constantly with a whisk. When the contents begin to simmer (at 185°F), remove the pan from the heat and let cool thoroughly.

3. Pour the cooled contents in the mixer, add the mascarpone, mix it all for a few moments. Place the contents in a hermetically sealed container and let it cool in the fridge for 5 to 6 hours.

4. Just under an hour before eating, pour the contents into the ice cream maker and let it set. Collect the mascarpone gelato when it is set, place it in a storage container, and eat it right away, or cover it with plastic wrap and store it in the freezer until ready to serve.

Gorgeous . . . and good, too!
Before making the gelato, break 7 or 8 cookies into large pieces with a spoon, soak in coffee, and harden in the freezer. When the gelato is ready, add cookie pieces into the ice cream maker. Serve in a cup, sprinkled with a few pinches of bitter cocoa.

For an even smoother, more velvety gelato
Add the following ingredients, combining them with half of the cold milk: ⅛ cup dextrose, ⅛ cup maltodextrin, ¼ tsp guar flour, ½ tsp soy lecithin, 1/16 cup glucose powder. Integrate this mixed milk at the start of step 2. The ingredients here are natural. They come from seeds or are very simple sugars. You can very easily find them either on the internet or in shops marketing kitchen goods and products. See p. 26 for more information.

AMARETTO GELATO

Amaretti are delicate little Italian cookies dusted with powdered almonds. Their smooth texture is inimitable.

Difficulty: easy
Serves: about 6 people
Preparation time: 15 minutes
Cooking time: 2 to 3 minutes
Chill time: 5 to 6 hours
In ice cream maker: about 40 minutes

INGREDIENTS:
3 oz Amorino amaretti + some for
  garnish
2½ cups milk
¼ cup light cream
⅛ cup powdered milk
1 cup powdered sugar

1. Before beginning the gelato, place the rather finely chopped amaretti cookies in the freezer. In a mixer, add the cold milk, cream, powdered milk, and sugar. Mix for a few moments. If you don't own a mixer, whisk these ingredients by hand in a mixing bowl.

2. Pour the contents into a saucepan. Heat, stirring constantly with a whisk. When the contents begin to simmer (at 185°F), remove the pan from the heat and let cool thoroughly.

3. Place the contents in a hermetically sealed container and, if possible, let it cool in the fridge for 5 or 6 hours.

4. Just under an hour before serving dessert, pour the contents into the ice cream maker and let it set. When the gelato is set, add the chopped cookies. Place the gelato in a storage container, then garnish it with a few whole or crushed cookies. Eat it right away, or cover it with plastic wrap and store it in the freezer until ready to serve.

Gorgeous . . . and good, too!
Offer the amaretti gelato in little bowls, sprinkled with a few nice whole, caramelized almonds.

For an even smoother, more velvety gelato
Add the following ingredients, combining them with half of the cold milk: ⅛ cup dextrose, ⅛ cup maltodextrin, ¼ tsp guar flour, ½ tsp soy lecithin, 1/16 cup glucose powder. Integrate this mixed milk at the start of step 2. The ingredients here are natural. They come from seeds or are very simple sugars. You can very easily find them either on the internet or in shops marketing kitchen goods and products. See p. 26 for more information.

CARAMEL GELATO WITH SALTED BUTTER

Topped with a hint of salt, the caramelized flavor of this gelato is simply irresistible. You can eat it as is, or served with fall fruits (figs, pears), fresh or lightly cooked in a frying pan.

Difficulty: easy
Serves: about 6 people
Preparation time: 15 minutes
Cooking time: 5 to 6 minutes
Chill time: 5 to 6 hours
In ice cream maker: about 40 minutes

INGREDIENTS:
1 cup powdered sugar
⅛ cup glucose powder
⅓ cup powdered milk
½ cup slightly salted butter
2½ cups milk
½ cup light cream
¼ cup liquid caramel
1 egg yolk
2 pinches salt
⅛ cup powdered milk

1. In a saucepan, add the sugar, glucose powder, ⅓ cup of powdered milk, and the butter cut into pieces. Bring to a boil and let cook up to 240°F. Remove saucepan from heat. In a mixer, add the cold milk, light cream, liquid caramel, egg yolk, salt, and powdered milk. Mix for a few moments. If you don't own a mixer, whisk these ingredients by hand in a mixing bowl.

2. Pour the contents into the saucepan containing the caramel with the salted butter. Heat, stirring constantly with a whisk. When the contents just begin to simmer (at 185°F), remove the pan from the heat and let cool thoroughly.

3. Place the contents in a hermetically sealed container and, if possible, let it cool in the fridge for 5 or 6 hours.

4. Just under an hour before serving dessert, pour the contents into the ice cream maker and let it set. When the gelato is set, place it in a storage container and eat it right away, or cover it with plastic wrap and store it in the freezer until ready to serve.

Gorgeous . . . and good, too!
Garnish your gelato with caramel slivers (p. 212), chopped nougats, caramelized pistachios (p. 204). Also consider caramel sauce (p. 216).

For an even smoother, more velvety gelato
Add the following ingredients, combining them with half of the cold milk: ⅛ cup dextrose, ⅛ cup maltodextrin, ¼ tsp guar flour, ½ tsp soy lecithin, and 1⁄16 cup glucose powder. Integrate this mixed milk at the start of step 2. The ingredients here are natural. They come from seeds or are very simple sugars. You can very easily find them either on the internet or in shops marketing kitchen goods and products. See p. 26 for more information.

AMORINO CHOCOLATE GELATO

There is an infinite number of recipes for chocolate gelato. Here's one whose smoothness and flavor are unique. You can personalize it by adding more or less cream, chocolate, or cocoa.

Difficulty: easy
Serves: about 6 people
Preparation time: 15 minutes
Cooking time: 2 to 3 minutes
Chill time: 5 to 6 hours
In ice cream maker: about 40 minutes

INGREDIENTS:
2 cups milk
¼ cup light cream
1 egg yolk
⅛ cup powdered milk
1¼ cups powdered sugar
1 cup powdered cocoa
1 oz chocolate (80 percent cacao or more)

1. In a mixer, add the cold milk, cream, egg yolk, powdered milk, sugar, and cocoa powder. Mix for a few moments. If you don't own a mixer, whisk these ingredients by hand in a mixing bowl.

2. Pour the contents into the saucepan; add the coarsely crushed chocolate. Heat, stirring constantly with a whisk. When the contents just begin to simmer and the chocolate is totally melted (at 185°F), remove the pan from the heat. Mix thoroughly again and let cool thoroughly.

3. Place the contents in a hermetically sealed container and, if possible, let it cool in the fridge for 5 or 6 hours.

4. Just under an hour before serving dessert, pour the contents into the ice cream maker and let it set. When the gelato is set, place it in a storage container and eat it immediately; it's at this very moment that it's irresistible. If it's not ready, cover it with plastic wrap and store it in the freezer until ready to serve.

Gorgeous . . . and good, too!
Serve this gelato as is or lightly sprinkled with chocolate shavings.

For an even smoother, more velvety gelato
Add the following ingredients, combining them with half of the cold milk: ⅛ cup dextrose, ⅛ cup maltodextrin, ¼ tsp guar flour, ½ tsp soy lecithin, 1/16 cup glucose powder. Integrate this mixed milk at the start of step 2. The ingredients here are natural. They come from seeds or are very simple sugars. You can very easily find them either on the internet or in shops marketing kitchen goods and products. See p. 26 for more information.

CREAM GELATO

This great Italian gelato classic seduces you with its beautiful ivory coating and an unmatched creaminess. Prepare it with a very high-quality light cream. Its flavor, rather discreet, gives permission to every personalized detail when you serve it. Be inventive!

Difficulty: easy
Serves: about 6 people
Preparation time: 15 minutes
Cooking time: 2 to 3 minutes
Chill time: 5 to 6 hours
In ice cream maker: about 40 minutes

INGREDIENTS:
1¾ cups milk
1½ cups light cream
4 egg yolks
⅛ cup powdered milk
1 cup powdered sugar

1. In a mixer, add the cold milk, light cream, egg yolks, powdered milk, and sugar. Mix for a few moments. If you don't own a mixer, whisk these ingredients by hand in a mixing bowl.

2. Pour the contents into the saucepan. Heat, stirring constantly with a whisk. When the contents just begin to simmer (at 185°F), remove the pan from the heat. Mix finely again and let cool thoroughly.

3. Place the contents in a hermetically sealed container and, if possible, let it cool in the fridge for 5 or 6 hours.

4. Just under an hour before serving dessert, pour the contents into the ice cream maker and let it set. When the gelato is set, place it in a storage container and eat it immediately; it's at this very moment that it's irresistible. If it's not ready, cover it with plastic wrap and store it in the freezer until ready to serve.

Gorgeous . . . and good, too!
Serve this gelato with chocolate sauce (p. 214), caramel (p. 216), a fruit coulis (p. 210), cooked fruits (p. 34), or slightly chilled. Also consider caramelized nuts (p. 204). At step 2, you can flavor the contents by heating it and adding a vanilla bean folded in two, a lemon peel, or a few coffee beans.

For an even smoother, more velvety gelato
Add the following ingredients, combining them with half of the cold milk: ⅛ cup dextrose, ⅛ cup maltodextrin, ¼ tsp guar flour, ½ tsp soy lecithin, 1/16 cup glucose powder. Integrate this mixed milk at the start of step 2. The ingredients here are natural. They come from seeds or are very simple sugars. You can very easily find them either on the internet or in shops marketing kitchen goods and products. See p. 26 for more information.

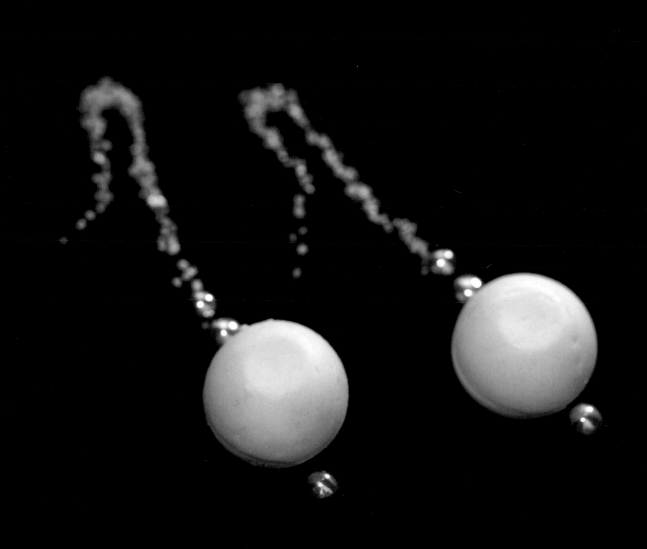

AMARENA (SOUR CHERRY) GELATO

Sour cherries are an inescapable part of the Italian gelato tradition. These little cherries cooked in syrup add a very distinctive sweetness to numerous desserts. You can either incorporate them into the gelato or drop them in cups, at the last moment.

Difficulty: easy.
Serves: about 6 people
Preparation time: 15 minutes
Cooking time: 2 to 3 minutes
Chill time: 5 to 6 hours
In ice cream maker: about 40 minutes

INGREDIENTS:
1 jar Amarena sour cherries
2½ cups milk
½ cup light cream
2 egg yolks
⅛ cup powdered milk
1 cup powdered sugar

1. Drain the cherries, reserving juice. In a dish, combine the cherries with half of their syrup (keep the remainder for future use). Place them in the freezer for at least 1 to 2 hours.

2. In a mixer, add the cold milk, light cream, egg yolks, powdered milk, and sugar. Mix for a few moments. If you don't own a mixer, whisk these ingredients by hand in a mixing bowl.

3. Pour the contents into the saucepan. Heat, stirring constantly with a whisk. When the contents begin to simmer (at 185°F), remove the pan from the heat and let cool thoroughly.

4. Place the contents in a hermetically sealed container and, if possible, let it cool in the fridge for 5 or 6 hours.

5. Just under an hour before serving dessert, pour the contents into the ice cream maker and let it set. When the gelato is set, add the cherries and glazed syrup, place it in a storage container, and eat it immediately, or cover it with plastic wrap and store it in the freezer until ready to serve.

Gorgeous . . . and good, too!
Serve the cherry gelato in soup plates, in the shape of petals, with a few Amarenas and fresh cherries.

For an even smoother, more velvety gelato
Add the following ingredients, combining them with half of the cold milk: ⅛ cup dextrose, ⅛ cup maltodextrin, ¼ tsp guar flour, ½ tsp soy lecithin, ¹⁄₁₆ cup glucose powder. Integrate this mixed milk at the start of step 3. The ingredients here are natural. They come from seeds or are very simple sugars. You can very easily find them either on the internet or in shops marketing kitchen goods and products. See p. 26 for more information.

PIEDMONT HAZELNUT GELATO

Like any of these recipes, to pull off this gelato, you need really good ingredients. Lean toward the Piedmont hazelnut: its fruity flavor distinguishes it from all others and will give your gelato an unmatched flavor.

Difficulty: easy
Serves: about 6 people
Preparation time: 15 minutes
Cooking time: 2 to 3 minutes
Chill time: 5 to 6 hours
In ice cream maker: about 40 minutes

INGREDIENTS:
1½ cups milk
¼ cup light cream
1 egg yolk
⅛ cup powdered milk
¾ cup powdered sugar
3 oz shelled and finely crushed
  hazelnuts

1. In a mixer, add the cold milk, light cream, egg yolk, powdered milk, and sugar. Mix for a few moments. If you don't own a mixer, whisk these ingredients by hand in a mixing bowl.

2. Pour the contents into the saucepan. Heat, stirring constantly with a whisk. When the contents just begin to simmer (at 185°F), remove the pan from the heat and let cool thoroughly.

3. Place the contents in a hermetically sealed container and, if possible, let it cool in the fridge for 5 or 6 hours.

5. Just under an hour before serving dessert, add the finely ground hazelnuts to the contents, then pour it into the ice cream maker and let it set. Collect the gelato when it sets, place it in a storage container, and eat it immediately, or cover it with plastic wrap and store it in the freezer until ready to serve.

Good . . . and gorgeous, too!
Serve the hazelnut gelato with a few whole hazelnuts, or some *tuiles* (baked wafer cookies) covered with chopped and toasted hazelnuts. You can also prepare the gelato as it is and add *crema di gianduja* (an Italian chocolate hazelnut spread) into the ice cream maker only at the last moment, thus creating a superb marbled effect.

For an even smoother, more velvety gelato
Add the following ingredients, combining them with half of the cold milk: ⅛ cup dextrose, ⅛ cup maltodextrin, ¼ tsp guar flour, ½ tsp soy lecithin, ¹⁄₁₆ cup glucose powder. Integrate this mixed milk at the start of step 2. The ingredients here are natural. They come from seeds or are very simple sugars. You can very easily find them either on the internet or in shops marketing kitchen goods and products. See p. 26 for more information.

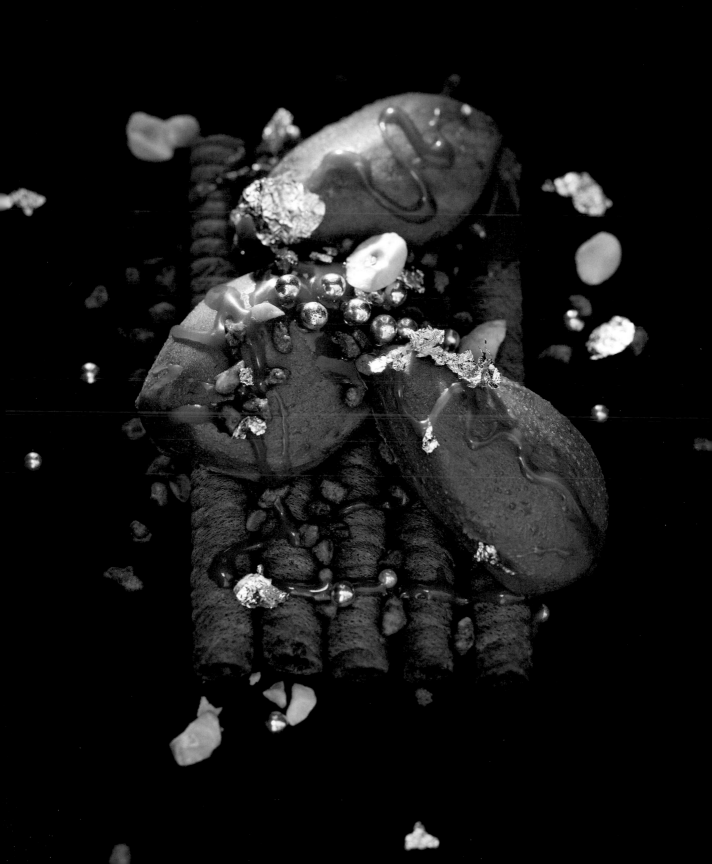

MILK CHOCOLATE GELATO

Here, the gelato is prepared with milk chocolate. Offer it to the kids on their birthday, as a treat. They'll be very excited!

Difficulty: easy
Serves: about 6 people
Preparation time: 15 minutes
Cooking time: 2 to 3 minutes
Chill time: 5 to 6 hours
In ice cream maker: about 40 minutes

INGREDIENTS:
2½ cups milk
¼ cup light cream
1 egg yolk
⅛ cup powdered milk
1 cup powdered sugar
¼ cup powdered cocoa

Garnish (optional): 1 cup
  shaved chocolate (80 percent or
  more cacao)

1. In a mixer, add the cold milk, cream, egg yolk, powdered milk, sugar, and powdered cocoa. Mix for a few moments. If you don't own a mixer, whisk these ingredients by hand in a mixing bowl.

2. Pour the contents into the saucepan. Heat, stirring constantly with a whisk. When the contents just begin to simmer (at 185°F), remove the pan from the heat. Mix finely again and let cool thoroughly.

3. Place the contents in a hermetically sealed container and, if possible, let it cool in the fridge for 5 or 6 hours.

4. Just under an hour before serving dessert, pour the contents into the ice cream maker and let it set. When the gelato is set, place the gelato in a storage container and eat it immediately: it's at this very moment that it's perfectly smooth. If you're not ready to eat it, cover it with plastic wrap and store it in the freezer until ready to serve.

Gorgeous . . . and good, too!
Serve the milk chocolate gelato garnished with chocolate shavings, cold minced hazelnuts, chocolate or multicolor sprinkles, toasted slivered almonds, or chocolate Chantilly cream (p. 206).

For an even smoother, more velvety gelato
Add the following ingredients, combining them with half of the cold milk: ⅛ cup dextrose, ⅛ cup maltodextrin, ¼ tsp guar flour, ½ tsp soy lecithin, 1/16 cup glucose powder. Integrate this mixed milk at the start of step 2. The ingredients here are natural. They come from seeds or are very simple sugars. You can very easily find them either on the internet or in shops marketing kitchen goods and products. See p. 26 for more information.

COFFEE GELATO

In Italy, coffee is truly a religion. Not surprising, then, that coffee gelati are so flavorful. The production technique is simple: the infusion of the coffee in the milk before preparing the gelato. Thanks to the wide variety of coffee available, you can vary the flavors.

Difficulty: easy
Serves: about 6 people
Preparation time: 15 minutes
Baking time: 2 to 3 minutes
Chill time: 5 to 6 hours
In ice cream maker: about 40 minutes

INGREDIENTS:
¾ cup milk
½ cup light cream
1 egg yolk
⅛ cup powdered milk
1 cup powdered sugar
1½ cups *ristretto* (espresso)

1. In a mixing bowl, add the cold milk, cream, egg yolk, and powdered milk and sugar. Stir the mixture well with a whisk in order to totally disperse the egg yolk and the sugar in the liquid.

2. Pour the contents into a saucepan. Heat, stirring constantly with a whisk, being careful not to let it boil. When the contents just begin to simmer (at 185°F), remove the pan from the heat and let cool thoroughly. Filter the contents in a conical strainer, then add the espresso. Combine well.

3. Place the contents in a hermetically sealed container and, if possible, let it cool in the fridge for 5 or 6 hours.

4. Just under an hour before serving dessert, pour the contents into the ice cream maker and let it set. When the gelato is set, eat it immediately, or cover it with plastic wrap and store it in the freezer.

Gorgeous . . . and good, too!
Serve the coffee gelato as is, or with a little melted chocolate, chocolate sauce (p. 214), coffee sauce (p. 218), homemade wafer cookies (p. 194), caramelized pistachios (p. 204), or a simple whipped cream (p. 206).

For an even smoother, more velvety gelato
Add the following ingredients, combining them with half of the cold milk: ⅛ cup dextrose, ⅛ cup maltodextrin, ¼ tsp guar flour, ½ tsp soy lecithin, ¹⁄₁₆ cup glucose powder. Integrate this mixed milk at the start of step 2. The ingredients here are natural. They come from seeds or are very simple sugars. You can very easily find them either on the internet or in shops marketing kitchen goods and products. See p. 26 for more information.

Tip
Lean toward mountain-grown Arabica coffee, with fruity flavors, either African or Central American.

STRACCIATELLA (CHOCOLATE CHIP) GELATO

This milk-based gelato with chocolate marbling is a delight where very different textures and flavors mingle: the softness and smoothness of the cream and milk sorbet with the crunch and strong taste of the chocolate.

Difficulty: easy
Serves: about 6 people
Preparation time: 15 minutes
Cooking time: 2 to 3 minutes
Chill time: 5 to 6 hours
In ice cream maker: about 40 minutes

INGREDIENTS:
3 oz dark chocolate
2½ cups milk
½ cup light cream
⅛ cup powdered milk
1 cup powdered sugar

1. In a warm double boiler, melt the dark chocolate. Don't let it heat too long.

2. In a mixer, add the cold milk, cream, powdered milk, and sugar. Mix for a few moments. If you don't own a mixer, whisk these ingredients by hand in a mixing bowl.

3. Pour the contents into a saucepan. Heat, stirring constantly with a whisk. When the contents begin to simmer (at a temperature of 185°F), remove the saucepan from the heat and let cool thoroughly.

4. Place the contents in a hermetically sealed container and, if possible, let it cool in the fridge for 5 or 6 hours.

5. Just under an hour before serving dessert, pour the contents into the ice cream maker, turn it on (follow the manufacturer's instructions), and let it set. When the gelato is well set and the guests are ready to eat, pour the chocolate in the gelato. Combine only as much as needed to get a marbled effect. Place the gelato in a storage container and eat it immediately, or cover it with plastic wrap and store it in the freezer until ready to serve.

Gorgeous . . . and good, too!
Serve this gelato accompanied with cocoa biscotti. You can also vary this classic by replacing the gelato with a sorbet and the melted chocolate with a coulis.

For an even smoother, more velvety gelato
Add the following ingredients, combining them with half of the cold milk: ⅛ cup dextrose, ⅛ cup maltodextrin, ¼ tsp guar flour, ½ tsp soy lecithin, ¹⁄₁₆ cup glucose powder. Integrate this mixed milk at the start of step 3. The ingredients here are natural. They come from seeds or are very simple sugars. You can very easily find them either on the internet or in shops marketing kitchen goods and products. See p. 26 for more information.

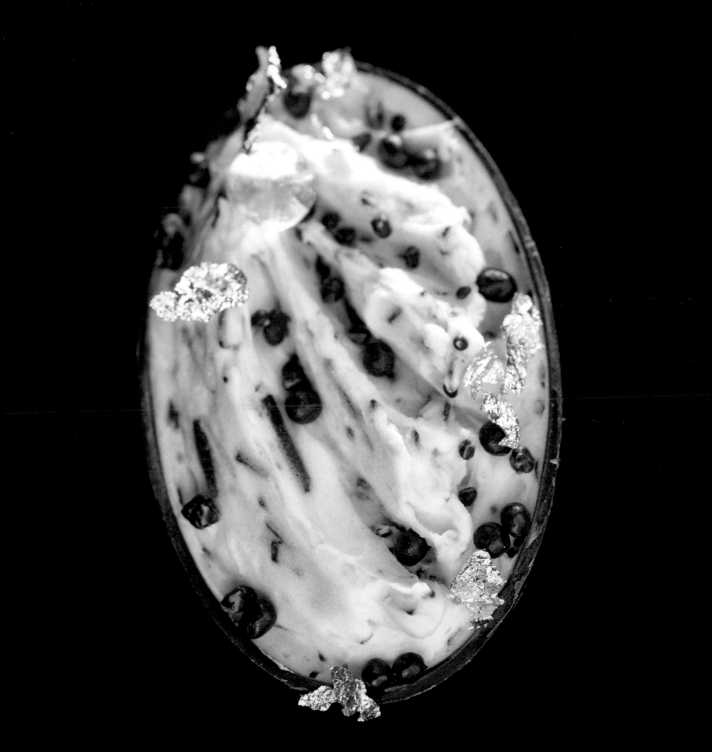

BOURBON VANILLA GELATO

Homemade bourbon vanilla gelato is as simple as it is subtle. The key to success resides in the choice of vanilla beans (which you'll find in fine markets) and how quickly you eat it after it's finished being prepared.

Difficulty: easy
Serves: about 6 people
Preparation time: 15 minutes
Cooking time: 2 to 3 minutes
Chill time: 5 to 6 hours
In ice cream maker: about 40 minutes

INGREDIENTS:
4 bourbon vanilla beans
2½ cups milk
½ cup light cream
⅛ cup powdered milk
1 cup powdered sugar

1. Cut the vanilla beans in two, lengthwise. With a small knife, scrape the insides of the half-beans to collect the little black seeds. In a mixer, add the black seeds, cold milk, light cream, powdered milk, and sugar. Mix for a few moments. If you don't own a mixer, whisk these ingredients by hand in a mixing bowl.

2. Pour the contents into a saucepan, add the vanilla bean halves. Heat, stirring constantly with a whisk. When the contents just begin to simmer (at 185°F), remove the pan from the heat and let cool thoroughly.

3. Place the contents in a hermetically sealed container and, if possible, let it cool in the fridge for 5 or 6 hours.

4. One hour before serving dessert, pour the contents into the ice cream maker (remove the vanilla bean halves) and let it set. When the gelato is well set, serve it immediately, or cover it with plastic wrap and store it in the freezer until ready to serve.

Gorgeous . . . and good, too!
Pair this gelato with a few drops of nice rum or Armagnac. Otherwise, consider whipped cream, melted chocolate, or chocolate shavings. Strawberries or raspberries are equally welcome.

For an even smoother, more velvety gelato
Add the following ingredients, combining them with half of the cold milk: ⅛ cup dextrose, ⅛ cup maltodextrin, ¼ tsp guar flour, ½ tsp soy lecithin, 1⁄16 cup glucose powder. Integrate this mixed milk at the start of step 2. The ingredients here are natural. They come from seeds or are very simple sugars. You can very easily find them either on the internet or in shops marketing kitchen goods and products. See p. 26 for more information.

FIOR DI LATTE (FRESH MILK CHEESE) GELATO

The taste of this relatively plain gelato makes it a remarkable base. You can embellish in a thousand ways: with sauces, fruits, zabaglione, liqueurs, etc. Everything, or nearly everything, is possible with fior di latte gelato. What's more, kids adore it.

Difficulty: easy
Serves: about 6 people
Preparation time: 1 hour
Cooking time: 2 to 3 minutes
Chill time: 5 to 6 hours
In ice cream maker: about 40 minutes

INGREDIENTS
2½ cups milk
½ cup light cream
¼ cup powdered milk
1 cup powdered sugar
½ cup unsweetened condensed
  milk.

1. In a mixer, add the cold milk, cream, powdered milk, sugar, and condensed milk. Mix for a few moments. If you don't own a mixer, whisk these ingredients by hand in a mixing bowl.

2. Pour the contents into a saucepan. Heat, stirring constantly with a whisk, being careful not to let it boil. When the contents just begin to simmer (at 185°F), remove the pan from the heat and let cool thoroughly. Chill in the fridge for 5 to 6 hours.

3. Pour the contents into the ice cream maker and let it set. When the gelato is set, serve it immediately; if it's not ready, place it in a storage container, cover it with plastic wrap, and store it in the freezer.

Gorgeous . . . and good, too!
With this gelato, allow yourself every combination and every audacity. Top it with sauces (p. 197), cooked fruits (p. 34), caramelized nuts (p. 204), Amorino colored (tapioca) pearls, or Amorino balsamic vinegar.

For an even smoother, more velvety gelato
Add the following ingredients, combining them with half of the cold milk: ⅛ cup dextrose, ⅛ cup maltodextrin, ¼ tsp guar flour, ½ tsp soy lecithin, ⅟₁₆ cup glucose powder. Integrate this mixed milk at the start of step 2. The ingredients here are natural. They come from seeds or are very simple sugars. You can very easily find them either on the internet or in shops marketing kitchen goods and products. See p. 26 for more information.

COCONUT GELATO

This gelato with a hint of exotic, creamy coconut taste is pleasing to everyone who enjoys coconut. It is rather rich, and you'll enjoy preparing it in the fall or in winter, a good time of year to pair it with other exotic fruits.

Difficulty: easy
Serves: about 6 people
Preparation time: 15 minutes
Cooking time: 2 to 3 minutes
Chill time: 5 to 6 hours
In ice cream maker: about 40 minutes

INGREDIENTS:
1¾ cups milk
½ cup light cream
⅛ cup powdered milk
1 cup powdered sugar
¾ cup coconut milk
⅓ cup powdered coconut

1. In a mixer, add the cold milk, light cream, powdered milk, and sugar. Mix for a few moments. If you don't own a mixer, whisk these ingredients by hand in a mixing bowl.

2. Pour the contents into a saucepan. Heat, stirring constantly with a whisk. When the contents just begin to simmer (at 185°F), remove the pan from the heat and let cool thoroughly. Add the coconut milk and the powdered coconut.

3. Place the contents in a hermetically sealed container and, if possible, let it cool in the fridge for 5 or 6 hours.

4. Just under an hour before serving dessert, pour the contents into the ice cream maker and let it set. When the gelato is well set, serve it immediately, or cover it with plastic wrap and store it in the freezer until ready to serve.

Gorgeous . . . and good, too!
Pair this coconut gelato with melted white chocolate, or diced mango, lychees, or passion fruit pulp. You can also top it with a few drops of coconut cream.

For an even smoother, more velvety gelato
Add the following ingredients, combining them with half of the cold milk: ⅛ cup dextrose, ⅛ cup maltodextrin, ¼ tsp guar flour, ½ tsp soy lecithin, ¹⁄₁₆ cup glucose powder. Integrate this mixed milk at the start of step 2. The ingredients here are natural. They come from seeds or are very simple sugars. You can very easily find them either on the internet or in shops marketing kitchen goods and products. See p. 26 for more information.

GLAZED CHESTNUT GELATO

Chestnut cream is a choice ingredient for preparing a unique gelato. Topped with a little dash of Armagnac, it earns universal approval! Prepare it in the fall and top it with figs and other seasonal fruits.

Difficulty: easy
Serves: about 6 people
Preparation time: 15 minutes
Cooking time: 2 to 3 minutes
Chill time: 5 to 6 hours
In ice cream maker: about 40 minutes

INGREDIENTS:
4 oz glazed chestnut fragments
2½ cups milk
¼ cup light cream
⅔ cup powdered sugar
⅛ cup powdered milk
¾ cup chestnut cream
4 tbsp Armagnac

1. Place the chestnut fragments in the freezer. In a mixer, add the cold milk, cream, sugar, and powdered milk. Mix for a few moments. If you don't own a mixer, whisk these ingredients by hand in a mixing bowl.

2. Pour the contents into a saucepan. Heat, stirring constantly with a whisk. When the contents just begin to simmer (at 185°F), remove the pan from the heat and let cool thoroughly. Mix the contents with the chestnut cream.

3. Place the contents in a hermetically sealed container and, if possible, let it cool in the fridge for 5 or 6 hours.

4. Just under an hour before serving dessert, pour the contents into the ice cream maker and let it set. When the gelato is set, add the glazed chestnut fragments and Armagnac, then place it in a storage container and eat it immediately, or cover it with plastic wrap and store it in the freezer until ready to serve.

Gorgeous . . . and good, too!
Top your chestnut gelato with more chestnut fragments, a caramel sauce (p. 216), or fresh fig quarters, as is or sautéed in the frying pan.

For an even smoother, more velvety gelato
Add the following ingredients, combining them with half of the cold milk: ⅛ cup dextrose, ⅛ cup maltodextrin, ¼ tsp guar flour, ½ tsp soy lecithin, 1/16 cup glucose powder. Integrate this mixed milk at the start of step 2. The ingredients here are natural. They come from seeds or are very simple sugars. You can very easily find them either on the internet or in shops marketing kitchen goods and products. See p. 26 for more information.

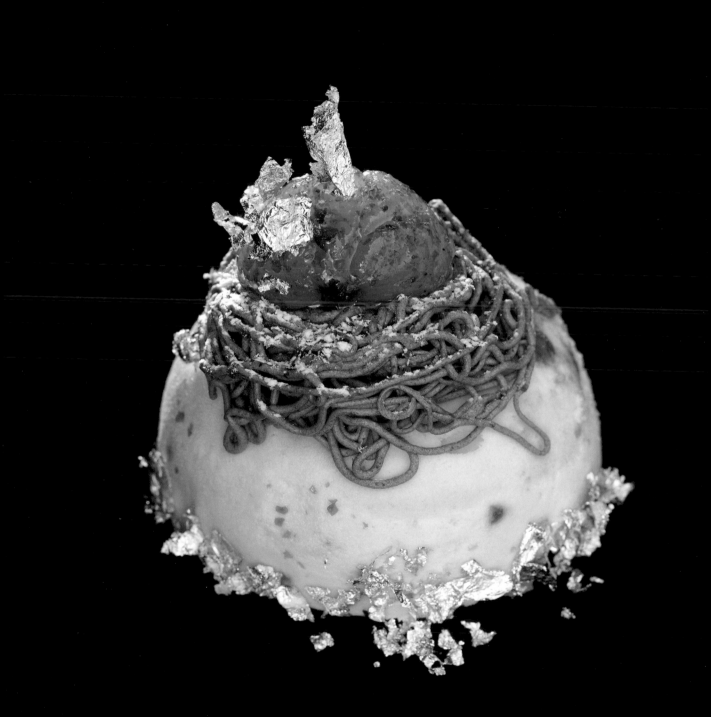

DULCE DE LECHE GELATO

This recipe has become a great classic in South America and Spain. It needs to be said that its inimitable flavor is approved unanimously by gourmets. And by food lovers, who often partner it with spice cookie gelato (p. 78).

Difficulty: easy
Serves: about 6 people
Preparation time: 15 minutes
Cooking time: 2 to 3 minutes
Chill time: 5 to 6 hours
In ice cream maker: about 40 minutes

INGREDIENTS:
3 cups milk
¼ cup light cream
⅛ cup powdered milk
½ cup powdered sugar
1 cup dulce de leche

1. In a mixer, add the cold milk, cream, powdered milk, and sugar. Mix for a few moments. If you don't own a mixer, whisk these ingredients by hand in a mixing bowl.

2. Pour the contents into a saucepan. Heat, stirring constantly with a whisk. When the contents just begin to simmer (at 185°F), remove the pan from the heat and let cool thoroughly. Then add the dulce de leche.

3. Place the contents in a hermetically sealed container and, if possible, let it cool in the fridge for 5 or 6 hours.

4. Just under an hour before serving dessert, pour the contents into the ice cream maker and let it set. When the gelato is set, place it in a storage container and eat it immediately, or cover it with plastic wrap and store it in the freezer until ready to serve.

Gorgeous . . . and good, too!
Serve this gelato as is, with a tablespoon of crème fraîche and a few caramel slivers (p. 212). Also offer it in crunchy *tulipes*, or dessert shells (p. 182).

For an even smoother, more velvety gelato
Add the following ingredients, combining them with half of the cold milk: ⅛ cup dextrose, ⅛ cup maltodextrin, ¼ tsp guar flour, ½ tsp soy lecithin, ¹⁄₁₆ cup glucose powder. Integrate this mixed milk at the start of step 2. The ingredients here are natural. They come from seeds or are very simple sugars. You can very easily find them either on the internet or in shops marketing kitchen goods and products. See p. 26 for more information.

ALMOND GELATO

The nutty flavor of almonds creates a delicious, decadent dessert for any occasion. Enjoy this garnished with caramelized almonds to enhance the already scrumptious flavor.

Difficulty: easy
Serves: about 6 people
Preparation time: 15 minutes
Cooking time: 7 to 8 minutes
Chill time: 5 to 6 hours
In ice cream maker: about 40 minutes

INGREDIENTS:
a small handful of caramelized
  almonds (p. 204)
3 cups milk
¼ cup light cream
1 egg yolk
⅛ cup powdered milk
¾ cup powdered sugar
¾ cup almond paste

1. For this recipe, make your almond paste: combine ¾ cup of well-flavored almond powder with ¾ cup of powdered sugar, then add a lightly beaten egg white. Form a tube that you will place in plastic wrap until ready to use.

2. Place the caramelized almonds in the freezer for 1 to 2 hours.

3. In a mixer, add the cold milk, cream, egg yolk, powdered milk, and sugar. Mix for a few moments. If you don't own a mixer, whisk these ingredients by hand in a mixing bowl.

4. Pour the contents into a saucepan. Heat, stirring constantly with a whisk. When the contents begin to simmer (at 185°F), remove from the heat and let cool thoroughly. Combine the contents with the almond paste.

5. Place the contents in a hermetically sealed container and, if possible, let it cool in the fridge for 5 or 6 hours.

6. Just under an hour before serving dessert, pour the contents into the ice cream maker and let it set. When the gelato is set, add the caramelized almonds, then place it in a storage container and eat it immediately, or cover it with plastic wrap and store it in the freezer until ready to serve.

Gorgeous . . . and good, too!
Serve this gelato with chocolate sauce (p. 214), caramel sauce (p. 216), a fruit coulis (p. 210), or cooked fruits (p. 34). Also consider other caramelized nuts.

For an even smoother, more velvety gelato
Add the following ingredients, combining them with half of the cold milk: ⅛ cup dextrose, ⅛ cup maltodextrin, ¼ tsp guar flour, ½ tsp soy lecithin, ¹⁄₁₆ cup glucose powder. Integrate this mixed milk at the start of step 3. The ingredients here are natural. They come from seeds or are very simple sugars. You can very easily find them either on the internet or in shops marketing kitchen goods and products. See p. 26 for more information.

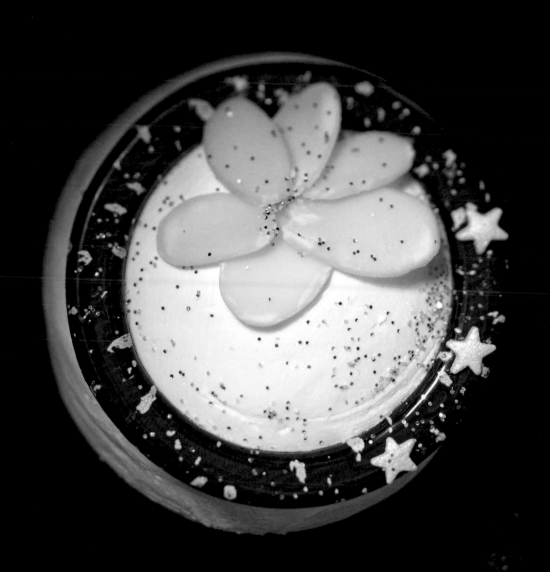

SPICE COOKIE GELATO

This gelato, one of the most surprising, will astonish all your guests every time. It is an ideal fall recipe, a comforting gelato, when the weather starts to get colder. Ideally churn it one hour before eating it: it will seem even more flavorful.

Difficulty: easy
Serves: about 6 people
Preparation time: 15 minutes
Cooking time: 2 to 3 minutes
Chill time: 5 to 6 hours
In ice cream maker: about 40 minutes

INGREDIENTS:
2½ cups milk
¼ cup light cream
⅛ cup powdered milk
¾ cup powdered sugar
½ cup spice cookie dough

1. In a mixer, add the cold milk, light cream, powdered milk, and sugar. Mix for a few moments. If you don't own a mixer, whisk these ingredients by hand in a mixing bowl.

2. Pour the contents into a saucepan. Heat, stirring constantly with a whisk. When the contents begin to simmer (at 185°F), remove the pan from the heat and let cool thoroughly.

3. Pour the cooled contents into the mixer, add the spice cookie dough, mix it all for just under a minute. You can mix by hand, but it's easier to use a mixer because the spice cookie dough can be quite dense sometimes. Place the contents in a hermetically sealed container and, if possible, let it cool in the fridge for 5 or 6 hours.

4. Just under an hour before serving dessert, pour the contents into the ice cream maker and let it set. Collect the gelato when it is set, place it in a storage container and eat it immediately, or cover it with plastic wrap and store it in the freezer until ready to serve.

Good . . . and gorgeous, too!
Place some small bowls in the freezer 30 minutes before filling them with spice cookie gelato. Garnish them with coarsely crushed spice cookie crumbs and a few sparse bitter dark chocolate shavings.

For an even smoother, more velvety gelato
Add the following ingredients, combining them with half of the cold milk: ⅛ cup dextrose, ⅛ cup maltodextrin, ¼ tsp guar flour, ½ tsp soy lecithin, ¹⁄₁₆ cup glucose powder. Integrate this mixed milk at the start of step 2. The ingredients here are natural. They come from seeds or are very simple sugars. You can very easily find them either on the internet or in shops marketing kitchen goods and products. See p. 26 for more information.

PISTACHIO GELATO

Sicilian pistachios are a delicacy that connoisseurs have appreciated for a long time. Crushed into a paste, they bring to the gelato a smoothness and a flavor that are literally inimitable.

Difficulty: easy
Serves: about 6 people
Preparation time: 15 minutes
Cooking time: 2 to 3 minutes
Chill time: 5 to 6 hours
In ice cream maker: about 40 minutes

INGREDIENTS:
2½ cups milk
¼ cup light cream
1 egg yolk
⅛ cup powdered milk
1 cup powdered sugar
4 oz finely blended Sicilian
  pistachios

1. In a mixer, add the cold milk, light cream, egg yolk, powdered milk, and sugar. Mix for a few moments. If you don't own a mixer, whisk these ingredients by hand in a mixing bowl.

2. Pour the contents into a saucepan. Heat, stirring constantly with a whisk. When the contents begin to simmer (at 185°F), remove the pan from the heat and let cool thoroughly.

3. Pour the cooled contents into the mixer, add the pistachios. Mix for just under a minute. Place the contents in a hermetically sealed container and, if possible, let it cool in the fridge for 5 or 6 hours.

4. Just under an hour before serving dessert, pour the contents into the ice cream maker and let it set. Collect the gelato when it is set, place it in a storage container and eat it immediately, or cover it with plastic wrap and store it in the freezer until ready to serve. You can add some whole shelled pistachios, at the last moment, when the gelato is ready to be removed from the ice cream maker.

Good . . . and gorgeous, too!
Place some small bowls in the freezer 30 minutes before filling them with pistachio gelato petals. Top with caramelized pistachios (p. 204) or a few crumbs of coarsely crushed Amorino amaretti (p. 48).

For an even smoother, more velvety gelato
Add the following ingredients, combining them with half of the cold milk: ⅛ cup dextrose, ⅛ cup maltodextrin, ¼ tsp guar flour, ½ tsp soy lecithin, 1/16 cup glucose powder. Integrate this mixed milk at the start of step 2. The ingredients here are natural They come from seeds or are very simple sugars. You can very easily find them either on the internet or in shops marketing kitchen goods and products. See p. 26 for more information.

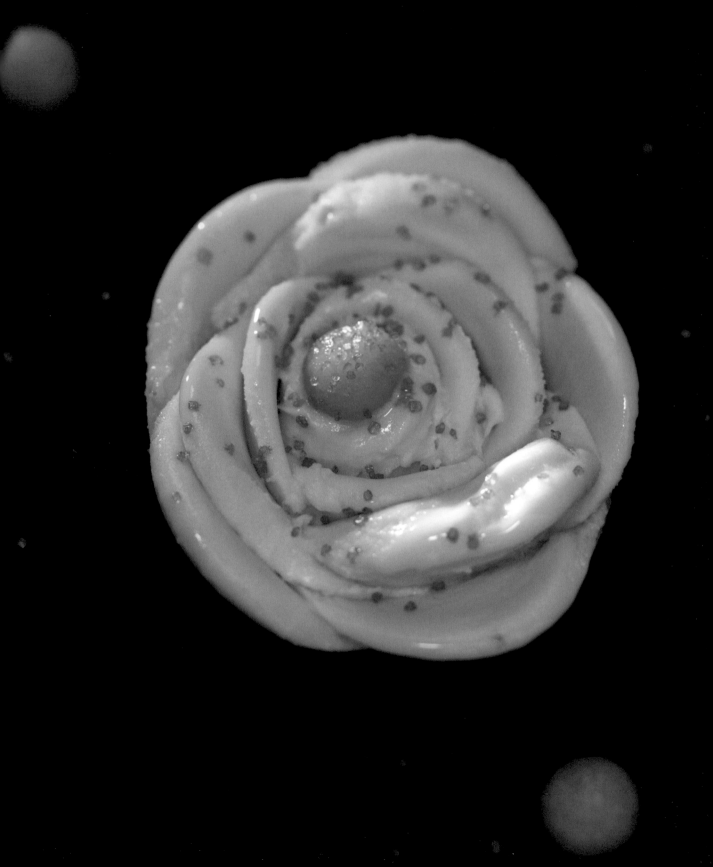

SORBET RECIPES
- Mango, lemon, raspberry, orange, black currant, and more! -

Italian sorbets, as close as possible to fruit

While gelato is a basic symbol of the Italian tradition of frozen desserts, sorbets occupy their own special place in Italian culture.

The simple tasting of an Italian sorbet lets you comprehend all the details. The texture: always thin, smooth, and rich; the flavor: that of a fruit and uniquely that. The pleasant texture of Italian sorbets can be explained as it can for gelati, by the temperature at which you taste them (p. 18). Their very flavor is the direct result of two extremely simple principles: putting in as many fruits as possible and not including any air in the preparation. In effect, in most of the recipes, the proportion of fruits is often greater than two-thirds of all of the ingredients! So it's not surprising that a mango sorbet resembles rather accurately the fruit from which it's derived. Then, when the sorbet is prepared in the ice cream maker, it is "beaten" delicately, not excessively, so that no air be included in its volume, which would accordingly diminish its flavor . . .

But let's stop a moment to discuss the quality of the fruits you should use to make a good sorbet. They should be, in a word, flawless. Freshness must be the benchmark: fruits that are mediocre, dry, withered, or not ripe enough will never produce a good sorbet, no matter how hard you try! You must use the best, the ripest, the sweetest, and the juiciest. How can you test this? Very simply: taste them . . .

MANGO SORBET

There is mango . . . and then there's mango! Look for the Alphonso variety, which is easily recognized by its yellow skin and its distinctive rather elongated shape. You can also choose peeled and pitted mangoes sold frozen, which are delicious.

Difficulty: easy
Serves: for 1 quart of sorbet, about 6 people
Preparation time: 15 minutes
In ice cream maker: about 40 minutes

INGREDIENTS:
22 oz mango flesh
⅙ cup lemon juice
1 cup sugar syrup (p. 32)
¼ cup water

1. In a mixer, add the mango flesh, lemon juice, sugar syrup, and water. Blend it all finely.

2. If need be, pass the resulting coulis through a fine strainer.

3. Pour the mango contents into the ice cream maker and let it set. Collect the sorbet and eat it immediately, or cover it with plastic wrap and store it in the freezer until ready to serve.

Good . . . and gorgeous, too!
Offer the mango sorbet in cups or well-chilled glasses. Or on soup plates with fine slices of peeled mangoes, marinated with a little Vermentino di Sardegna (wine) and a hint of chopped mint.

For an even smoother, more velvety sorbet
Add the following ingredients, blending them with half of the mango flesh: ⅛ cup dextrose, ⅛ cup maltodextrin, ¼ tsp guar flour, 1/16 cup glucose powder. Bring this preparation to a simmer (without letting it boil), then integrate it with the syrup. The ingredients here are natural. They come from seeds or are very simple sugars. You can very easily find them either on the internet or in shops marketing kitchen goods and products. See p. 26 for more information.

BANANA SORBET

Here, once again, the choice of fruits makes all the difference. To prevent the sorbet from being too dark or from lacking flavor, avoid bananas that are too green or too ripe. Choose bananas that are very yellow but whose peel is not spotted with black, a sign of advanced ripening.

Difficulty: easy
Serves: for 1 quart of sorbet, about
6 people
Preparation time: 20 minutes
Cooking time: 2 to 3 minutes
In ice cream maker: about 40 minutes

INGREDIENTS:
1 lb peeled bananas
juice of 2 lemons
1¼ cups powdered sugar
1½ cups water

1. Blend the bananas finely with the lemon juice in the food processor. Do not omit this step; if you do, the banana purée will turn black.

2. In a saucepan, add the sugar and water. Bring to a boil, let cool, strain syrup.

3. In a mixer, add the syrup and the banana purée. Blend to combine these ingredients thoroughly.

4. Pour the banana contents into the ice cream maker and let it set. Collect the sorbet as soon as it sets and eat it immediately, or cover it with plastic wrap and store it in the freezer until ready to serve. But in this case, it will harden quickly and thus lose a large part of its appeal. To avoid this, refer to the heading "For an even more velvety and smoother sorbet," to follow.

Good . . . and gorgeous, too!
Offer the banana sorbet with melted chocolate, Chantilly cream (p. 206), fruit coulis (p. 210), caramel (p. 216), seasonal fruits . . .

For an even smoother, more velvety sorbet
Add the following ingredients, blending them with half of the banana flesh: ⅛ cup dextrose, ⅛ cup maltodextrin, ¼ tsp guar flour, 1/16 cup glucose powder. Bring this preparation to a simmer (without letting it boil), then integrate it with the syrup. The ingredients here are natural. They come from seeds or are very simple sugars. You can very easily find them either on the internet or in shops marketing kitchen goods and products. See p. 26 for more information.

PASSION FRUIT SORBET

This recipe demands a little work and patience, but it's worth all the trouble. The resulting sorbet is as creamy as it is refreshing and flavorful.

Difficulty: intermediate
Serves: for 1 quart of sorbet, about 6 people
Preparation time: 25 minutes
In ice cream maker: about 40 minutes

INGREDIENTS:
4½ lbs fresh passion fruit to make 3 cups juice
1 cup sugar syrup (p. 32)

1. Cut the fruits in two. With a spoon, hollow them out. Strain the flesh of the passion fruits so you only collect the juice. You should end up with 3 cups. In the mixer, add the passion fruit juice and the sugar syrup. Blend it all finely.

2. Pour the contents into the ice cream maker and let it set. Collect the sorbet as soon as it sets and eat it immediately, or cover it with plastic wrap and store it in the freezer until ready to serve.

Good . . . and gorgeous, too!
Serve this sorbet in chilled soup plates, with a hint of strawberry coulis (p. 210) and a few exotic fruits (mango, guava, pitaya . . .). To prepare this sorbet, you can also calculate the quantities of ingredients by observing the following proportion: 25 percent fruit juice and 75 percent syrup.

For an even smoother, more velvety sorbet
Add the following ingredients, blending them with half of the juice of the passion fruits: ⅛ cup dextrose, ⅛ cup maltodextrin, ¼ tsp guar flour, 1/16 cup glucose powder. Bring this preparation to a simmer (without letting it boil), then integrate it with the syrup. The ingredients here are natural. They come from seeds or are very simple sugars. You can very easily find them either on the internet or in shops marketing kitchen goods and products. See p. 26 for more information.

SORRENTO LEMON SORBET

Sorrento lemon sorbet is eaten as a dessert, but also during the meal, to mark a pause between two courses. You can also prepare it with limes, and even add some yuzu juice to it.

Difficulty: easy
Serves: for 1 quart of sorbet, about 6 people
Preparation time: 15 minutes
Cooking time: 2 to 3 minutes
In ice cream maker: about 40 minutes

INGREDIENTS:
1 cup sugar
2 cups water
zest of ¼ organic lemon (without the white skin)
1 cup Sorrento lemon juice

1. In a saucepan, add the sugar, water, and coarsely chopped zests. Bring to a boil, let cool, strain syrup.

2. In a mixer, add the lemon juice and sugar syrup. Blend to combine these ingredients thoroughly.

3. Pour the lemon contents into the ice cream maker and let it set. Collect the sorbet as soon as it sets and eat it immediately, or cover it with plastic wrap and store it in the freezer until ready to serve. But in this case, it's going to harden quickly. To avoid this, refer to the heading "For an even more velvety and smoother sorbet," to follow.

Good . . . and gorgeous, too!
Serve this sorbet with candied lemon and orange zests, lemon quarters, a hint of vodka. To vary the flavor, you can infuse a few sprigs of lemongrass in the syrup.

For an even smoother, more velvety sorbet
Add the following ingredients, blending them with half of the juice of the passion fruits: ⅛ cup dextrose, ⅛ cup maltodextrin, ¼ tsp guar flour, ⅟₁₆ cup glucose powder. Bring this preparation to a simmer (without letting it boil), then integrate it with the syrup. The ingredients here are natural. They come from seeds or are very simple sugars. You can very easily find them either on the internet or in shops marketing kitchen goods and products. See p. 26 for more information.

STRAWBERRY SORBET

Change up the taste of this sorbet by using different varieties of strawberries.

Difficulty: easy
Serves: for 1 quart of sorbet, about 6 people
Preparation time: 15 minutes
In ice cream maker: about 40 minutes

INGREDIENTS:
2.2 lbs fresh or frozen strawberries (1½ lbs pulp)
2 tbsp lemon juice
1 cup sugar syrup (p. 32)
¼ cup water

1. Remove the stems, cut and blend the strawberries finely, then strain the resulting mass through a fine strainer to eliminate all the seeds. You have to end up with 1½ lbs of pulp.

2. In a mixer, add the strawberry pulp, lemon juice, syrup, and water. Blend it all finely.

3. Pour the strawberry contents into the ice cream maker and let it set. Collect the sorbet as soon as it sets and eat it immediately, or cover it with plastic wrap and store it in the freezer until ready to serve.

Good . . . and gorgeous, too!
Serve as is or "in the Italian style" with a little dash of Amorino balsamic vinegar . . .

For an even smoother, more velvety sorbet
Add the following ingredients, blending them with half of the strawberry pulp: ⅛ cup dextrose, ⅛ cup maltodextrin, ¼ tsp guar flour, 1/16 cup glucose powder. Bring this preparation to a simmer (without letting it boil), then integrate it with the syrup. The ingredients here are natural. They come from seeds or are very simple sugars. You can very easily find them either on the internet or in shops marketing kitchen goods and products. See p. 26 for more information.

MELON SORBET

For a good melon sorbet, choose the ripest possible fruits and, as opposed to other varieties, lean toward cantaloupe, which has a sweet and refreshing flavor.

Difficulty: easy
Serves: for 1 quart of sorbet, about 6 people
Preparation time: 15 minutes
In ice cream maker: about 40 minutes

INGREDIENTS:
3 melons (1½ lbs flesh, no skin or seeds)
⅙ cup lemon juice
1 cup sugar syrup (p. 32)
¼ cup water

1. Open the melons, remove the seeds and the skin. Weigh the flesh: you need 1½ lbs of it to make the recipe. In a mixer, add the melon flesh, lemon juice, sugar syrup, and water. Blend it all finely.

2. If your mixer isn't very powerful and some lumps remain, pass the coulis through a fine strainer.

3. Pour the melon contents into the ice cream maker and let it set. Collect the sorbet and eat it immediately, or cover it with plastic wrap and store it in the freezer until ready to serve. But don't delay because it will harden pretty quickly.

Good . . . and gorgeous, too!
Offer the melon sorbet in cups or well-chilled glasses. Top it with diced melon and a dash of chilled port. You can also pair it with black currant berries, wild strawberries . . .

For an even smoother, more velvety sorbet
Add the following ingredients, blending them with half of the melon flesh: ⅛ cup dextrose, ⅛ cup maltodextrin, ¼ tsp guar flour, 1/16 cup glucose powder. Bring this preparation to a simmer (without letting it boil), then integrate it with the syrup. The ingredients here are natural. They come from seeds or are very simple sugars. You can very easily find them either on the internet or in shops marketing kitchen goods and products. See p. 26 for more information.

RASPBERRY SORBET

Raspberry sorbet is one of the most refreshing. Here, it is prepared with lime juice. To change it up, try your own combinations: raspberry-strawberry, raspberry-black currant, raspberry-red currant. In this last instance, you'll likely have to sweeten the recipe a bit more.

Difficulty: easy
Serves: for 1 quart of sorbet, about 6 people
Preparation time: 15 minutes
In ice cream maker: about 40 minutes

INGREDIENTS:
2.2 lbs fresh or frozen raspberries (1½ lbs of pulp)
⅙ cup lime juice
1 cup sugar syrup (p. 32)
¼ cup water

1. Blend the raspberries finely, then strain the resulting mass through a fine strainer to eliminate all the seeds. You need 1½ lbs of pulp.

2. In a mixer, add the raspberry pulp, lime juice, sugar syrup, and water. Blend it all finely.

3. Pour the raspberry contents into the ice cream maker and let it set. Collect the sorbet as soon as it sets and eat it immediately, or cover it with plastic wrap and store it in the freezer until ready to serve.

Good . . . and gorgeous, too!
Offer this sorbet with fresh raspberries, red currants, black currant berries, or mint leaves. Otherwise, a vanilla sauce (p. 202) or a hint of Chantilly cream (p. 206) will be welcome.

For an even smoother, more velvety sorbet
Add the following ingredients, blending them with half of the raspberry pulp: ⅛ cup dextrose, ⅛ cup maltodextrin, ¼ tsp guar flour, ¹⁄₁₆ cup glucose powder. Bring this preparation to a simmer (without letting it boil), then integrate it with the syrup. The ingredients here are natural. They come from seeds or are very simple sugars. You can very easily find them either on the internet or in shops marketing kitchen goods and products. See p. 26 for more information.

ORGANIC PEAR SORBET

For connoisseurs, this sorbet, made with organic ingredients, is unique. Prepared with totally ripe Williams or Conference pears, it develops a warm and seductive flavor.

Difficulty: intermediate
Serves: for 1 quart of sorbet, about 6 people
Preparation time: 20 minutes
Cooking time: 30 minutes
In ice cream maker: about 40 minutes

INGREDIENTS:
3.3 lbs organic powdered sugar
6 cups water
1 organic vanilla bean
3.3 lbs organic pears
2 organic lemons

1. In a saucepan, add the sugar, water, and vanilla bean cut in two lengthwise. Bring to a boil, then let simmer. Let cook 30 minutes, remove from the heat, and let cool.

2. Peel the pears, hollow them with an apple corer, cut them in two lengthwise. Rub them generously with a lemon cut in two. Combine them with 1 cup of syrup and the juice of 1 lemon. Pour the pear contents into the ice cream maker and let it set. Collect the sorbet as soon as it sets and eat it immediately, or cover it with plastic wrap and store it in the freezer until ready to serve. But in this case, it's going to harden pretty quickly and will thus lose a big part of its softness and its creaminess. To avoid this, refer to the heading "For an even more velvety and smoother sorbet," to follow.

Good . . . and gorgeous, too!
Offer this sorbet in cups or well-chilled glasses, with a few dark chocolate shavings, as few crumbs of biscotti, a drop of pear liqueur, a little caramel sauce (p. 216), or a few caramelized nuts (p. 204).

For an even smoother, more velvety sorbet
Add the following ingredients, blending them with half of the pear flesh: $\frac{1}{8}$ cup dextrose, $\frac{1}{8}$ cup maltodextrin, $\frac{1}{4}$ tsp guar flour, $\frac{1}{16}$ cup glucose powder. Bring this preparation to a simmer (without letting it boil), then integrate it with the syrup. The ingredients here are natural. They come from seeds or are very simple sugars. You can very easily find them either on the internet or in shops marketing kitchen goods and products. See p. 26 for more information.

ORANGE SORBET

Orange sorbet is one of the most refreshing types. If, moreover, you prepare it with blood oranges, its beautiful crimson color will astonish all your guests and will make it even more tempting!

Difficulty: easy
Serves: for 1 quart of sorbet, about 6 people
Preparation time: 20 minutes
Cooking time: 2 to 3 minutes
In ice cream maker: about 40 minutes

INGREDIENTS:
1 cup powdered sugar
3 cups juice of blood oranges
zest of ½ organic blood orange
  (without the white skin)

1. In a saucepan, add the sugar, 1¼ cups of orange juice, and coarsely chopped zest. Bring to a boil, let cool, strain syrup. In a mixer, add the syrup and remaining orange juice. Blend to combine these ingredients thoroughly.

2. Pour the orange contents into the ice cream maker and let it set. Collect the sorbet as soon as it sets and eat it immediately, or cover it with plastic wrap and store it in the freezer until ready to serve. But in this case, it's going to harden quickly and will thus lose a great part of its appeal. To avoid this, refer to the heading "For an even more velvety and smoother sorbet," to follow.

Good . . . and gorgeous, too!
Offer this sorbet with orange quarters, candied orange sauce, or a few finely cut young verbena leaves.

For an even smoother, more velvety sorbet
Add the following ingredients, blending them with half of the orange juice: ⅛ cup dextrose, ⅛ cup maltodextrin, ¼ tsp guar flour, 1/16 cup glucose powder. Bring this preparation to a simmer (without letting it boil), then integrate it with the syrup. The ingredients here are natural. They come from seeds or are very simple sugars. You can very easily find them either on the internet or in shops marketing kitchen goods and products. See p. 26 for more information.

BLACK CURRANT SORBET

The sensuous flavor of black currant produces truly unique sorbets that real food lovers especially appreciate. The preparation is a bit long and a tad messy. Wear an apron, or else your clothes will be forever stained!

Difficulty: intermediate
Serves: for 1 quart of sorbet, about
6 people
Preparation time: 30 minutes
Cooking time: 2 to 3 minutes
In ice cream maker: about 40 minutes

INGREDIENTS:
1½ lbs black currants (1 lb
  strained pulp)
1½ cups powdered sugar
1¼ cups water

1. Blend the currants finely in the food processor. Strain the resulting paste through a fine strainer to eliminate skin and seeds. You need 1 lb of pulp.

2. In a saucepan, add the sugar and the water. Bring to a boil, let cool completely.

3. In a mixer, add the syrup and the black currant pulp. Blend to combine these ingredients thoroughly.

4. Pour the black currant contents into the ice cream maker and let it set. Collect the sorbet as soon as it sets and eat it immediately: it's now that it's the most flavorful. If it's not ready, cover it with plastic wrap and store it in the freezer until ready to serve.

Good . . . and gorgeous, too!
Offer this sorbet as is, with a few berries (black currants, red currants, blueberries), or with another less robust sorbet (strawberry, for instance) to balance its flavor.

For an even smoother, more velvety sorbet
Add the following ingredients, blending them with half of the black currant pulp: ⅛ cup dextrose, ⅛ cup maltodextrin, ¼ tsp guar flour, 1/16 cup glucose powder. Bring this preparation to a simmer (without letting it boil), then integrate it with the syrup. The ingredients here are natural. They come from seeds or are very simple sugars. You can very easily find them either on the internet or in shops marketing kitchen goods and products. See p. 26 for more information.

RECIPES FOR ICES AND SMOOTHIES

- Lemon, grapefruit, almond, coffee . . . -

Ices and smoothies, more recipes and more pleasures

In Italy, people like to eat smoothies and ices on the terrace at the end of the day, in the matchless comfort of summer evenings . . . To take advantage of the coolness of these very thirst-quenching delicacies, make some for yourself!

———————

Semisolid or semiliquid, ices and smoothies can be drunk slowly or eaten with a spoon. Ices are, in fact, sorbets that you freeze without blending them. So, the water contained in the preparation freezes little by little to form large ice crystals. This is what creates its appeal: an incredible sensation of coolness joined with delicate flavors—lemon, lime, grapefruit, orange, tea . . . The combinations are virtually limitless.

Smoothies are something else entirely. These are finely blended mixtures of gelato (or sorbets) and coffee, tea, fruit juice, infusion, etc. The result is a very thirst-quenching drink that is made slightly thick due to the cold that the gelato (or sorbet) releases during the blending. Likewise, the possible flavor combinations are endless. It isn't hard to personalize these preparations according to tastes and desires.

Ices, like smoothies, get warm very quickly. To fully appreciate their refreshing side, you must eat them quickly, as soon as they are served. Offer them in chilled glasses that you have left in the freezer for 1 to 2 hours.

SORRENTO LEMON ICE

Preparing lemon ice in the summer is a must. Very simple to make, it doesn't require an ice cream maker. Also consider preparing it with the henceforth-famous yuzu, which is a fragrant citrus fruit that has been adopted by many renowned chefs.

Difficulty: easy
Serves: for 1 pint (16 fl oz) of ice, 4 to 6 people
Preparation time: 15 minutes
Cooking time: 2 to 3 minutes
In freezer: about 2 hours

INGREDIENTS:
¾ cup powdered sugar
⅚ cup water
zest of ¼ organic Sorrento lemon
 (without the white skin)
¾ cup lime juice

1. In a saucepan, add the sugar, water, and coarsely chopped lemon zests. Bring to a boil, let cool, strain the syrup.

2. In a mixer, add the lime juice and strained sugar syrup. Mix to combine these ingredients thoroughly.

3. Pour the contents into a shallow metal storage container. Ideally, the mixture shouldn't be more than 1 inch deep. Place the storage container in the freezer. Let the contents freeze little by little, stirring it regularly every 10 minutes, and a bit more often at the end, when it begins to solidify.

4. As soon as the ice is ready, serve it.

Good . . . and gorgeous, too!
Offer this lemon ice very simply, in frosted glasses. Garnish with a little mint, 1 or 2 zests of candied lime. You can also top it with a few drops of iced vodka.

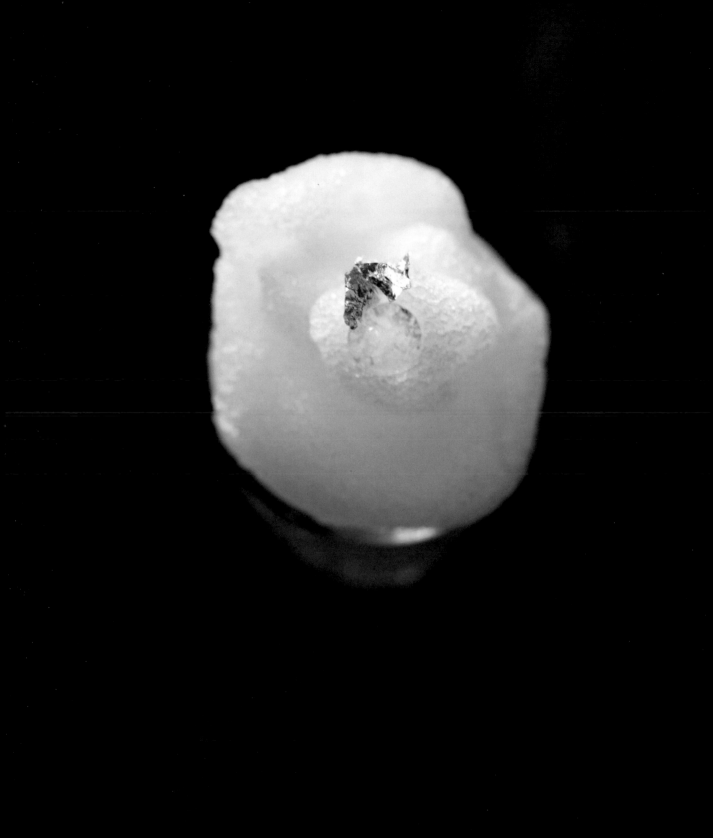

CANDIED GRAPEFRUIT ICE

For this ice, use pink grapefruits, bursting with juices and flavors. To give it a dash of bitterness, replace a third of the quantity of recommended juice with the juice of a yellow grapefruit.

Difficulty: easy
Serves: for 1 pint (16 fl oz) of ice, 4 to 6 people
Preparation time: 15 minutes
Cooking time: 2 to 3 minutes
Chill time: 24 hours
Time in freezer: about 2 hours

INGREDIENTS:
ZESTS: zest of ½ organic grapefruit (without the white skin)
¾ cup powdered sugar
¼ cup water
ICE: 2 cups pink grapefruit juice.

1. ZESTS: boil them for a few seconds in a little pot of water. Drain them. In a saucepan, add them whole with the sugar and water. Bring to a boil, let cool. Let soak for a day.

2. ICE: In a mixer, add the grapefruit juice, the cooked syrup of the zests, and the finely chopped zests. Mix to combine these ingredients thoroughly. Taste the contents before freezing it: add more sugar to your syrup according to the ripeness of the fruits.

3. Pour the grapefruit contents into a shallow metal storage container. Ideally, the ice shouldn't be more than 1 inch thick. Place the storage container in the freezer. Let the contents freeze little by little, stirring it regularly every 10 minutes, and a bit more often at the end, when it begins to solidify.

4. As soon as the ice is ready, serve it.

Good . . . and gorgeous, too!
Offer the candied grapefruit ice in frosted glasses, with, perhaps, a few grapefruit quarters, a tablespoon of strawberry coulis (p. 210) or, simply, as is . . .

ALMOND ICE

For this ice, which is beloved in Southern Italy, choose whole almonds of top quality, Italian if possible, and bought at a specialty food store. This particularly refined dessert will pair well with a few biscotti or some still-warm amaretti.

Difficulty: easy
Serves: for 1 pint (16 fl oz) of ice, 4 to 6 people
Preparation time: 15 minutes
Cooking time: 2 to 3 minutes
In freezer: about 2 hours

INGREDIENTS:
Almonds: ¼ lb almonds
Ice: ⅚ cup almond milk
½ cup almond paste
⅓ cup powdered sugar

1. ALMONDS: Lightly brown the coarsely crushed almonds in an oven heated at medium heat, taking care not to burn them. They must take on a slightly golden color. Remove them from the heat, place them in a dish, let cool.

2. ICE: In a mixer, add the almond milk and the almond paste. Mix in order to combine these ingredients well. Place this mixture in a saucepan, add the roasted almonds and the sugar. Bring to a simmer while stirring. Remove from the heat, cover, let cool. Strain the ingredients, keep the almonds for future use (cakes, cookies).

3. Pour the almond contents into a shallow metal storage container. Ideally, the ice shouldn't be more than 1 inch thick. Place the storage container in the freezer. Let the contents freeze little by little, stirring it regularly every 10 minutes, and a bit more often at the end, when it begins to solidify.

4. As soon as the ice is ready, serve it.

Good . . . and gorgeous, too!
Garnish the ice with some whole caramelized almonds (p. 204).

COFFEE SMOOTHIE

The Amorino coffee smoothie has become a classic in the category. Eat it in our shops or prepare it at home based on the following recipe.

Difficulty: easy
Serves: 2
Preparation time: 5 minutes

INGREDIENTS:
4 espressos (½ to ⅔ cups)
  prepared (in the espresso maker)
  with a strong and fruity Arabica
  with a dash of acidity
1¾ cups coffee sorbet (p. 62) or
  an Amorino coffee gelato

1. Prepare the espressos, let them cool a moment.

2. In a mixer, add the coffee gelato (separated in a few pieces if it's still hard) and the cooled coffees. Blend until you have a nice texture, a bit thick. Don't blend too much; otherwise, the gelato will totally melt.

Good . . . and gorgeous, too!
You might want to garnish the smoothies with some liqueur-dipped coffee beans, a little vanilla whipped cream (p. 206), a few dark chocolate shavings (more than 70 percent cacao), a trace of cinnamon . . .

RASPBERRY SMOOTHIE

For this recipe, the blender is indispensable. You can make numerous versions of raspberry smoothies. Here's one where raspberry sorbet and raspberries form a most thirst-quenching mixture.

Difficulty: easy
Serves: about 4 people
Preparation time: 20 minutes
Time in freezer: about 2 hours

INGREDIENTS:
RASPBERRIES:
1 lb fresh raspberries

SMOOTHIE:
4 tbsp raspberry sorbet (p. 100)
4 level tbsp. powdered sugar
a few drops of lemon juice
⅚ cup very cold mineral water

1. RASPBERRIES: spread out the raspberries on a plate, then place them in the freezer for at least 2 hours.

2. SMOOTHIE: Place blender container in the freezer about 30 minutes before using. Shortly before serving your smoothie, remove the blender and add the raspberries, sorbet, sugar, lemon juice, and very cold mineral water. Blend as finely as possible, until you get a nice bright pink paste. Taste. If the smoothie is too thick, add a little water. If it's not sweet enough, add some sugar. Serve it immediately with a straw.

Good . . . and gorgeous, too!
You might want to garnish the smoothie with some nice whole raspberries.

ALFONSO MANGO SMOOTHIE

Here, the smoothie is prepared with the flesh of the mango and a lemon-flavored black tea. Depending on the ripeness of the fruits, you may need to add some sugar or some infusion. Choose Indian mangoes with a pale-yellow color and elongated form. Very juicy, they're perfect for this recipe.

Difficulty: easy
Serves: about 4 people
Preparation time: 20 minutes
Cooking time: 2 to 3 minutes
Time in freezer: about 2 hours 45 minutes

INGREDIENTS:
MANGOES AND INFUSION:
4 Alphonso mangoes
2 cups water
1 level tbsp. black tea
juice of 1 lime
4 level tbsp powdered sugar

SMOOTHIE:
4 tbsp Amorino mango sorbet
   (p. 88)

1. MANGOES AND INFUSION: peel the mangoes, remove the pits. Cut the flesh into pieces, then put them on a plate and place in the freezer for 1½ to 2 hours. Separately, bring some water to a simmer in a saucepan. Add the tea, remove from heat. Allow to infuse 3 to 4 minutes. Strain, let cool thoroughly.

2. Take ⅝ cup of this infusion, add the lime juice, combine well, and place in the freezer for about 45 minutes (the mixture must almost be frozen).

3. SMOOTHIE: Place blender container in the freezer about 30 minutes before using. Shortly before serving your smoothie, remove the blender and add the infusion, mango flesh, and mango sorbet. Blend as finely as possible, until you get a nice yellow paste. Taste. Serve without delay in large glasses with a straw.

Good . . . and gorgeous, too!
Place a few small mango dices, even a little passion fruit pulp on the smoothie. A very distinct trace of spices is also a possibility, or a little mint or finely trimmed verbena, which will produce a rather refined garnish.

CLASSIC CREATIONS

- Dessert shell with red berries and mint, tri-flavored frozen bombe . . . -

Traditional recipes

Log cakes, dessert shells, soufflés, and frozen bombes, among others, are part of the somewhat-forgotten great Italian tradition of frozen desserts.

Certainly, experienced gourmands know these refined specialties well, but often, most people only have access to these desserts through their industrial, commercialized versions in supermarkets. But nothing will ever equal preparing homemade desserts using the most artisanal method possible to discover or rediscover all of their subtle notes. From the familiar flavor of the vanilla parfait to the lightness of the iced soufflé by way of the spectacular tri-flavored frozen bombe, expand your repertoire and learn, in a few rather simple techniques, to pull off succulent desserts, truly celebrating gelato and sorbets. Step out of the ordinary with the following recipes and dare to make the most beautiful and freshest creations imaginable!

FROZEN CARAMEL LOG CAKE

To save some time, prepare this house specialty with Amorino vanilla gelato. But you can also make the recipe with a fior di latte gelato (p. 68), spice cookie gelato (p. 78), or even one of the sorbets (p. 83).

Difficulty: difficult
Serves: 6 to 8 people
Preparation time: 1 hour 30 minutes
Cooking time: 2 hours 25 minutes
Time in freezer: at least 5 hours

SPECIAL EQUIPMENT:
electric mixer
rectangular pastry mold of about
8 x 12 x 3 inches
tray or sheet of correct
dimensions on which to place it
parchment paper
pastry bags
gas torch for crèmes brûlées

INGREDIENTS:
CAKE:
5 egg whites
1 pinch salt
1 cup powdered sugar
1 cup almond powder
¼ cup cornstarch
¼ cup powdered sugar

OTHER COMPONENTS:
meringues (p. 148)
bourbon vanilla gelato (p. 66)
vanilla syrup
very cold caramel sauce (p. 216)
caramel bits (p. 212)

1. Form mini meringues of about 1 inch long on a sheet. Cook them in the oven preheated at 230°F for 2 hours. Let cool, then keep in fridge. Place the pastry mold and its support in the freezer. Preheat the oven to 300°F. Whip the egg whites with the salt in the mixer. Cover the baking sheet with parchment paper. Trace with a pencil a 10 x 14-inch rectangle. In a bowl, combine the powdered sugar, almond powder, and cornstarch thoroughly. Add the sugar to the whipped egg whites, beat them very firmly. With a spatula, add the almond-sugar-cornstarch mixture, delicately and with precision, without letting the whites flatten.

2. Put the batter in a large pastry bag. Lay a rectangle of the batter following the drawing made on the parchment paper and garnish the inside of the rectangle with batter. Bake in the oven for 25 minutes. Remove the sheet from the oven, and let cool.

3. With a spoon, place the vanilla gelato in a pastry bag. With a serrated knife, cut the cake up to the dimensions of your mold and place it inside (don't forget to remove the parchment paper). With a brush, moisten it with vanilla syrup. Lay and spread flat a 1-inch-thick layer of vanilla gelato on the cake. On the top, distribute some mini meringues, pressing them lightly so that the surface is as flat as possible. Put back in the freezer for 1 hour.

4. Pour evenly a layer of caramel sauce on the top. Put it back in the freezer for at least 1 hour. To finish it, spread another layer of vanilla gelato so the level of your dessert is full to the brim of the mold you are using. Put back in the freezer for at least 3 hours.

5. With a gas torch, briefly reheat the walls of the mold and remove it. Cut up the rectangle of gelato into little 4 x 2-inch pieces. Sprinkle with caramel slivers, serve immediately.

FROZEN SOUFFLÉ WITH AMARETTO LIQUEUR

This spectacular dessert will impress all your guests. You have to prepare it in advance and serve it in its mold, like a "real" soufflé.

Difficulty: intermediate
Serves: about 6 people.
Preparation time: 40 minutes
Cooking time: 10 minutes
Time in freezer: at least 5 to 6 hours

SPECIAL EQUIPMENT:
parchment paper and rubber bands
food processor
soufflé mold 15 cm in diameter

INGREDIENTS:
2 bourbon vanilla beans
2 cups milk
3 cups powdered sugar
12 egg yolks
2 cups cold light cream
½ cup Amaretto

1. Surround the outside of the soufflé mold with 2 or 3 strips of parchment paper, securing them with rubber bands, for instance, for the purpose of raising the total height of the mold by about 1½ to 2 inches. Cut the vanilla beans in two lengthwise. With a small knife, scrape the insides of the half-beans to collect the little black seeds within. In a saucepan, add the little black seeds and the milk. Heat and whisk the milk, remove the saucepan from the heat, cover.

2. In a mixing bowl, add the sugar and egg yolks. Whip them in a food processor for about 1 minute. Add the hot vanilla milk and bean with the black seeds, combine briskly. Pour this preparation back in the saucepan. Cook at low heat, stirring constantly, as if you were preparing a custard. Above all, do not let boil.

3. When the preparation has thickened, remove the saucepan from the heat. Remove the vanilla beans. Pour the contents in the processor bowl and blend it on high for 5 to 6 minutes, then at medium for about 10 minutes.

4. Beat the cold light cream firmly. Delicately, add and combine the Amaretto and the whipped cream to the vanilla contents. Fill the mold to the brim, then slip it into the freezer. Let harden for at least 5 to 6 hours.

Good . . . and gorgeous, too!
Remove the strips of parchment paper and offer the soufflé in its mold. Serve it with a spoon, pairing it, for instance, with a caramel sauce (p. 216) or fresh or sautéed with a bit of butter. Of course, you can offer a small glass of Amaretto with the soufflé . . .

TRIFLAVORED FROZEN BOMBE

This dessert, descended from an ancient tradition, is spectacular once sliced: the color contrasts are as unique as they are appetizing. You will find the spherical mold you need in specialty food stores.

Difficulty: difficult
Serves: about 6 people
Preparation time: 2 hours
Cooking time: 10 minutes
Time in freezer: at least 2 hours, plus at least overnight

SPECIAL EQUIPMENT:
spherical or conical mold for a frozen bombe of about 1½ quarts
electric mixer
sauce thermometer

INGREDIENTS:
GELATO AND SORBET:
2 cups bourbon vanilla gelato (p. 66)
2 cups strawberry sorbet (p. 96) or another of your choosing

FROZEN BOMBE:
  6 egg yolks
1 cup powdered sugar
¼ cup cold water
⅝ cup cold light cream
¼ lb candied fruits

1. THE GELATO AND THE SORBET: place in a mold in the freezer for 15 minutes. Work separately on the gelato and the sorbet to make them suppler and more malleable. Line the inside of the mold with the vanilla gelato, in as uniform a layer as possible. Let harden a good hour in the freezer. Repeat the procedure, this time with strawberry sorbet, which should totally mask the vanilla gelato. Let harden 1 hour in the freezer.

2. THE FROZEN BOMBE: beat the yolks at medium so that they blanch and, little by little, swell, like stiff whites. During this time, add the sugar and the water in a saucepan. Bring to a boil. When the syrup reaches a temperature of 225 to 230°F, remove the saucepan from the heat and pour the hot syrup on the well-beaten yolks (and, above all, beating them constantly!). Set the beater to its maximum speed, then let cool like this for 5 minutes. Continue the cooling down, now beating the zabaglione at medium-slow, for 5 more minutes. Separately, beat the very cold light cream firmly. Combine the zabaglione with the light cream, add the chopped candied fruits.

3. THE FINAL TOUCH: pour the contents into the open space of the mold, until it is filled to the brim. Let harden in the freezer overnight.

4. Partially submerge the mold in a mixing bowl with warm water, then remove the bombe from the mold and onto a cold plate.

Good . . . and gorgeous, too!
Garnish the surface with your choice of whipped cream (p. 206), sauces (p. 197), candied fruits, bitter cocoa sprinkled with the help of a fine strainer . . .

HAZELNUT GELATO AND HAZELNUT COOKIE

Hazelnut lovers will savor this recipe, which features this succulent nut. Its fruity flavor sets it apart from all others.

Difficulty: easy
Serves: about 6 people
Preparation time: 35 minutes
Cooking time: 10 minutes

SPECIAL EQUIPMENT:
parchment paper

INGREDIENTS:
¾ cup soft butter
⅔ cup Demerara brown sugar
1 egg
1½ cups flour
⅓ cup powdered coconut
4 oz grated white chocolate
3 oz roasted and chopped
  hazelnuts
4 oz dehydrated cranberries
  (optional)
Piedmont hazelnut gelato (p. 58)

GARNISH (OPTIONAL):
caramelized hazelnuts (p. 204)

1. COOKIES: in a mixing bowl, combine the butter and sugar with a whisk. Add the egg, combine thoroughly. Add the flour, coconut, white chocolate, roasted hazelnuts, and cranberries. Combine for a few minutes. In squares of plastic wrap, form lumps of dough about 1½ inches in diameter, close the squares of wrap and let rest a moment in the fridge. Once the dough is hardened, take it out of the fridge and remove the plastic wrap. Line the baking sheet with parchment paper. Cut the lumps into slices ⅕ inch thick that you will set on the parchment paper. Cook them for 10 minutes in the oven preheated at 350°F. Remove the sheet from the oven, let cool.

2. THE GARNISH: in plates or cups, add the hazelnut gelato and some cookies. Top with a few caramelized hazelnuts. Serve without delay.

Good . . . and gorgeous!
The recipe also produces a spectacular result with almonds, walnuts, pistachios . . .

FROSTED DESSERT SHELL WITH RED BERRIES AND MINT

The delicate and crumbly tulip pastry forms a refined jewelry case for an assortment of gelatos and sorbets. Spectacular and delicate, this dessert will be the object of admiration of all your guests.

Difficulty: intermediate
Serves: about 6 people
Preparation time: 40 minutes
Cooking time: 10 minutes
Dough setting time: 2 hours

SPECIAL EQUIPMENT:
parchment paper

INGREDIENTS:
3 to 4 egg whites (120 g)
½ cup butter
1 vanilla bean
1 cup powdered sugar
1 cup sifted flour
strawberry sorbet (p. 96)
mango sorbet (p. 88)
bourbon vanilla gelato (p. 66)
⅝ lb red berries (strawberries, wild strawberries, red currants, black currants, raspberries)
raspberry coulis (p. 210)
a few mint leaves

1. Leave the egg whites at room temperature. Also, take the butter out of the fridge, let it soften thoroughly. It should have the consistency of face cream. Cut the vanilla bean in two lengthwise. With a small knife, scrape the insides of the half-beans to collect the little black seeds within.

2. In a mixing bowl, combine the soft butter with the vanilla seeds and powdered sugar. Add the whites, little by little, combining continually. Last, add the flour. Combine again. Let the dough rest in the fridge for 2 hours.

3. Preheat the oven at 350°F. Cover the baking sheet with parchment paper. Knead the dough to soften it. Lay 6 nice clumps of dough on the sheet, with lots of space between. Spread them with a spatula to make circles of about 4 inches in diameter. Put them in the oven for 8 to 10 minutes. Remove the dough circles from the oven, unstick them, place them in bowls, fitting them exactly, let cool.

4. When you serve the desserts, places the shells on plates. Place inside them an assortment of sorbets and gelatos in the shape of petals. Spread some red berries on top, coat with a little raspberry coulis, finish off the garnish with a hint of mint, serve immediately.

Good . . . and gorgeous, too!
Cook 1¾ cups of sugar in a saucepan with 4 to 5 tablespoons of water and a few drops of lemon juice to make a caramel sauce. Off the heat, blend into the caramel 7 oz of finely chopped hazelnuts, stirring with a spatula. Distribute the resulting hot crunch in 4 small bowls and, with half a lemon, spread it so it fits the bowls perfectly to get your shells. Let chill, garnish with sorbets, and top with raspberry coulis.

FROZEN BOURBON VANILLA PARFAIT

The technique for this dish lets you prepare delicious frozen desserts without an ice cream maker. It can be flavored with chocolate, cinnamon, or fruits. Here, the unique flavor of bourbon vanilla is front and center.

Difficulty: intermediate
Serves: 6 to 8 people
Preparation time: 40 minutes
Cooking time: about 15 minutes
Time in freezer: at least 5 to 6 hours

SPECIAL EQUIPMENT:
soufflé, a brioche, or a cake mold
electric beater
food processor

INGREDIENTS:
2 bourbon vanilla beans
1 cup milk
1 cup powdered sugar
6 egg yolks
1 cup cold light cream

1. Place the molds of your choice in the freezer. You can use a soufflé, a brioche, or a cake mold. In any case, the parfait is served out of the mold. Cut the vanilla beans in two lengthwise. With a small knife, scrape the insides of the half-beans to collect the little black seeds within. In a saucepan, add the vanilla beans and little black seeds and the milk. Heat and whisk the milk, remove the saucepan from the heat, cover.

2. In a mixing bowl, add the sugar and the egg yolks. Beat them for about 1 minute. Add the hot vanilla milk, combine briskly. Pour this preparation back in the saucepan. Cook at low heat, combining constantly, as if you were preparing a custard. Above all, do not let boil.

3. When the preparation has thickened, remove the saucepan from the heat. Remove the vanilla beans. Pour the contents in the processor bowl and blend it on high for 5 to 6 minutes, then at medium for about 10 minutes.

4. Beat the cold light cream firmly. Delicately, add and combine the whipped cream to the vanilla contents. Fill the mold, then slip it into the freezer. Let harden for at least 5 to 6 hours.

Good . . . and gorgeous, too!
For the presentation, take the molds out of the freezer, soak them for a few moments in a mixing bowl filled with tepid water. Turn the mold over and remove the contents onto a well-chilled plate. Top your parfait with whipped cream (p. 206), fruit coulis (p. 210), sauces (p. 197), cooked fruits (p. 34), or fresh fruits. Also consider Amorino colored tapioca pearls, crumbs of Amorino biscotti, a nice spoonful of Amorino *gianduja* (Italian chocolate hazelnut spread) . . .

YOGURT GELATO AND ROASTED FRUITS

Discover this subtle hot-cold harmony between juicy fruits and slightly tart yogurt gelato.

Difficulty: easy
Serves: about 6 people
Preparation time: 30 minutes
Cooking time: 15 to 20 minutes

SPECIAL EQUIPMENT:
parchment paper

INGREDIENTS:
1 bourbon vanilla bean
5 tbsp brown sugar
2 white peaches
2 yellow peaches
1 small mango
4 apricots
4 plums
a few rather firm strawberries
¼ cup melted butter
the juice of a large orange
yogurt gelato (p. 42)

1. Place some soup plates in the freezer. Preheat the oven at 425°F. Open the vanilla bean in two lengthwise. Collect the little seeds within and, in a bowl, combine them with the sugar.

2. Submerge the peaches for a few seconds in a saucepan of boiling water, then in cold water. Drain them, then peel them. Peel the mango, wash the apricots and the plums. Remove the stems from the strawberries, cut them in two.

3. Cut all these fruits to your liking, but rather in large pieces or quarters. Cover the baking sheet with a leaf of parchment paper. Spread the fruits on top. Sprinkle them with the vanilla sugar, baste with melted butter and the orange juice.

4. Put the fruits in the oven and bake for 15 minutes. If you want to brown them even more, remove them from the oven, then set the oven on the "broil" setting; put in the oven again, on the top rack, and let caramelize (be careful: depending on the oven, this procedure can go very quickly).

5. Distribute the gelato in plates, spread the roasted fruits all around, and on top, coat with cooking juice, serve immediately.

For a little variety
A good two hours before serving dessert, place a pastry circle 2¾ to 3¼ inches in diameter at the bottom of a cold soup plate. Fill it with softened yogurt gelato, level it, and put it back in the freezer to harden. Do the same for the other plates. Then, all there's left to do is add the cooked fruits . . .

Depending on the season, vary your fruits. Consider figs, apples, pears . . .

FROSTED ORANGES AND LEMONS

Prepare for yourself this childhood memory and discover (or rediscover) its delicious coolness. Imagine being able to prepare this thirst-quenching snack with tangerines, blood oranges, grapefruits.

Difficulty: easy
Serves: about 6 people
Preparation time: 35 minutes
Cooking time: 15 to 20 minutes
Time in freezer: at least 5 to 6 hours

SPECIAL EQUIPMENT:
pastry bag (optional)

INGREDIENTS:
6 lemons
6 oranges
orange sorbet (p. 104)
lemon sorbet (p. 92)

1. With a knife, section and take off the tops of the lemons and oranges. Cut up and make long cuts in the pulp, in the inside of the citrus fruits. With a spoon, empty them, taking care not to pierce the skin. Place the hollowed-out citrus fruits in the freezer for 5 or 6 hours.

2. With a spoon or a pastry bag, fill the citrus fruits with a generous portion of sorbet. Place the tops of the fruits on the sorbet, put back in the freezer for a little less than a half hour, then eat.

Good . . . and gorgeous, too!
Prepare the fruits frosted . . . surprise! Fill some hollowed-out oranges with strawberry sorbet (p. 96), for instance, then cover it with orange sorbet. Guaranteed results at the time of eating!

FROZEN NAPOLEON WITH HAZELNUTS, MERINGUE, VANILLA, AND RED BERRIES

Here's a recipe that requires a little time, work, and care, but whose result will compensate your efforts! Prepare this recipe for important occasions.

Difficulty: difficult
Serves: 6 to 8 people
Preparation time: 1 hour 30 minutes
Cooking time: 25 minutes
Time in freezer: at least 5 to 6 hours

SPECIAL EQUIPMENT:
electric beater
candy thermometer
pastry bag
rectangular pastry mold of about
8 x 12 x 3 inches
tray or sheet of correct
dimensions on which to place it

INGREDIENTS:
MERINGUE:
5 egg whites
1 pinch salt
1¾ cups powdered sugar
½ cup water

OTHER COMPONENTS:
cake (p. 132)
bourbon vanilla gelato (p. 66)
caramelized hazelnuts (p. 204)
   left in the freezer for 1 hour
strawberry or raspberry coulis
   (p. 210)
red berries (strawberries,
   raspberries, red currants, black
   currants, blueberries)

1. Prepare the cake as indicated on step 1 of the frozen log cake (p. 132). Separately, prepare the meringues: in a beater, whip the egg whites with the salt on slow speed. At the same time, boil the sugar and the water in a saucepan. When the temperature of the syrup reaches 225 to 230°F, pour it gently onto the well-whipped whites, beating them constantly. Continue beating until it's completely cooled. Place the meringue in a pastry bag. Form the meringues, in the shapes of your choice, but not much bigger than tangerines, on a sheet covered with parchment paper. Cook about 2 hours in the oven preheated at 225°F. When the meringues are very dry, take them out of the oven and let them cool. Crush 5 or 6 of them rather coarsely.

2. Cut up the cake to the dimensions of the mold and place it inside. Cover it with a 1-inch-thick layer of very softened vanilla gelato. Flatten the surface and place it in the freezer for 1 hour. Cover it with crushed meringues (no more than ½ inch), cover with 1 inch of vanilla gelato. Smooth and flatten the surface. Let settle a bit in the freezer (about 30 minutes). Cover

generously with caramelized (and very cold) hazelnuts. Push them very gently into the gelato. Let harden in the freezer for at least 2 hours.

Serve the napoleon whole or cut up into portions, pair it with a strawberry or raspberry coulis and a nice assortment of red berries.

For a little variety
Play with colors: replace the vanilla gelato with a mango sorbet (p. 88) and a passion fruit sorbet (p. 92). In winter or fall, replace the red berries with figs, pears, and apples sautéed in the frying pan and lightly caramelized . . .

HOMEMADE VANILLA AND MILK CHOCOLATE ESKIMO BARS

Rediscover the "true" flavor of a vanilla and chocolate Eskimo bar with this recipe that's simple and lots of fun to prepare. For a perfect result . . . ask the kids to help out!

Difficulty: easy
Serves: 6 to 8 people
Preparation time: 30 minutes
Cooking time: 3 to 4 minutes
Time in freezer: at least 5 to 6 hours

SPECIAL EQUIPMENT:
plastic Eskimo molds with shape and size of your choosing, pastry bag (optional)

INGREDIENTS:
bourbon vanilla gelato (p. 66)
14 oz chocolate (52 percent cacao)
1 cup milk
1 cup light cream
¼ cup butter
6 oz crushed caramelized hazelnuts (p. 204, optional)

1. Place the Eskimo molds in the freezer.

2. With a spoon or a pastry bag, fill the molds with vanilla gelato (be careful not to leave large air bubbles). Close the filled Eskimo molds and leave them in the freezer for 5 or 6 hours.

3. After this, prepare the coating. Grate or chop the chocolate. In a saucepan, add the milk, cream, and the butter cut into pieces. Heat. As soon as the mixture begins to rise, remove the saucepan from the heat. Add the chocolate at once, then combine until you get a bright liquid, uniform mass. Let cool. The coating is ready to be used when it is warm. Pour it into a deep container, where you can submerge the Eskimos (a measuring glass, for instance).

4. Remove the Eskimos. Dip a frozen Eskimo into the coating and remove immediately. Let the excess coating run off by (gently) shaking once or twice. Sprinkle with chopped hazelnuts, if you are using them. Place the Eskimos in the freezer immediately for about a half hour to let the coating harden, then eat them.

For a little variety
Prepare a coating with white chocolate: grate or chop 14 oz of white chocolate. In a saucepan, add 1 cup of cream, and ⅛ cup of butter cut into pieces. Heat. As soon as the mixture begins to rise, remove the saucepan from the heat. Add the chocolate at once, then combine until you get a uniform preparation. Let cool a moment before submerging the Eskimos in it.

Good to know
To get a very fine coating, add more milk: the more the coating is runny, the less it will stick to the Eskimos when you dip them in the chocolate.

FIOR DI LATTE (FRESH MILK CHEESE) GELATO, STRAWBERRIES, AND BALSAMIC VINEGAR

For this Italian marriage, choose a nice balsamic vinegar or a "cream of balsamic." For a beautiful presentation, place the plates or serving cups in the freezer so the gelato doesn't melt too quickly.

Difficulty: easy
Serves: about 6 people
Preparation time: 1 hour
Cooking time: 3 to 4 minutes

SPECIAL EQUIPMENT:
mixer
candy thermometer

INGREDIENTS:
GELATO:
3 cups milk
¼ cup light cream
1 egg yolk
⅕ cup powdered milk
1 cup powdered sugar
½ cup unsweetened condensed milk

FRUITS AND VINEGAR:
1 lb strawberries (Mara des Bois and Gariguette together, if possible)
2 tbsp powdered sugar
a few drops lemon juice
a few tbsp strawberry coulis (p. 210)
1 small bottle Amorino balsamic vinegar

1. GELATO: in a mixer, add the cold milk, cream, egg yolk, powdered milk, sugar, and condensed milk. Mix for a few moments. If you don't own a mixer, whisk these ingredients by hand in a mixing bowl. Pour the contents into a saucepan. Heat, stirring constantly with a whisk. When the contents begins to simmer (at 185°F), remove from the heat and let cool thoroughly. Pour the contents into the ice cream maker and let it set. When the gelato is set, place it in a storage container in the freezer.

2. FRUITS: place your cups or plates in the freezer. Wash the strawberries, remove the stems, cut them in two lengthwise. Place them in a bowl and, very gently, combine them with the sugar and lemon juice.

3. PRESENTATION: take the cups or plates out of the freezer. On the bottom, pour a little strawberry coulis. With 2 tablespoons soaked in the warm water, form 2 nice petals of fior di latte gelato. Place them side by side on the coulis. On top, spread some strawberries, then, delicately and with moderation, drip a few drops of balsamic vinegar. Serve immediately.

For a little variety
Also make this recipe with cream gelato (p. 54) or even vanilla (p. 66). Consider, as well, serving your strawberry sorbet (p. 96) with a few drops of vinegar.

For an even more velvety and smoother fior di latte gelato
Add the following ingredients, combining them with half of the cold milk: ¼ cup dextrose, ¼ cup maltodextrin, ¼ tsp guar flour, ½ tsp soy lecithin, ¹⁄₁₆ cup glucose powder. Integrate this mixed milk at the start of step 1. The ingredients here are natural. They come from seeds or are very simple sugars. You can very easily find them either on the internet or in shops marketing kitchen goods and products. See p. 26 for more information.

CREAM GELATO
WITH RED BERRIES

The distinctive tart flavor of red berries forms a delicious contrast with the smoothness of the cream gelato. A little touch of raspberry coulis brings these two flavors together and forms a refined combination . . . and it's easy to pull off.

Difficulty: easy
Serves: about 6 people
Preparation time: 1 hour
Cooking time: 3 to 4 minutes

SPECIAL EQUIPMENT:
mixer
fluted pastry bag

INGREDIENTS:
8 oz strawberries
1 tbsp. powdered sugar
a few drops of lime juice
4 oz raspberries
a few black currant berries
a few red currants and blueberries
cream gelato (p. 54)
a few tbsp raspberry coulis
　(p. 210)
a few Amorino colored (tapioca)
　pearls

1. Put some pretty glasses or cups in the freezer. Wash the strawberries, remove the stems, cut them in two lengthwise. In a bowl, combine the strawberries with the sugar and the lime juice. Sort out the other berries; eliminate, where appropriate, those you consider to be shriveled.

2. Place 8 or 10 tablespoons of gelato in a fluted pastry bag.

3. Very rapidly, spread some gelato on the bottom of the cold glasses or cups. Distribute the strawberries, their juice, and all the other berries on top. Top it all off with a well-chilled raspberry coulis. At the end, garnish the glasses with a few Amorino tapioca pearls.

Quick tip
If the use of the pastry bag puts you off, form some gelato petals with two spoons. Enhance this recipe by adding one teaspoon of very cold crème fraîche just before pouring the coulis.

AMORINO CREATIONS
- Tiramisu dish, dark chocolate affogato. . . -

Gustatory joy and pleasure
above all . . .

At Amorino, the pleasure of good things is a passion—
one of learning to select the best ingredients to use
in order to make original delicious desserts.

In this chapter, you're going to be able to pair the different gelato and sorbet recipes in this book and join them in numerous side dishes (sauces, fruits, caramelized fruits . . . see p. 197) to make desserts that are always original, delicious, and easy to make. You don't have to seek complexity to pull them off, quite the contrary: it is often the most obvious unions (affogato with dark chocolate) or the most natural (panna cotta dish) that meet with the most success. Remember, too, that the best dessert is the one you will have imagined yourself. Glean ideas here and there during the course of these pages and dare to invent your own creations. They will be, by definition . . . inimitable!

HOT-AND-COLD 100 PERCENT PISTACHIO: HOT AMARETTI AND GELATO

With this 100 percent pistachio recipe, discover the subtlety of joining "hot-and-cold," gelato and hot cookie.

Difficulty: easy
Serves: about 6 people
Preparation time: 20 minutes
Cooking time: 20 minutes
Chill time: overnight for the amaretti, if possible

SPECIAL EQUIPMENT:
electric beater
fluted pastry bag
parchment paper

INGREDIENTS:
HOT PISTACHIO AMARETTI:
1 oz slivered almonds
¾ cup almond powder
⅓ cup flour
1 cup powdered sugar
2 to 3 egg whites
1 tsp pistachio paste
powdered sugar
a few peeled Sicilian pistachios
  (for the garnish)

PISTACHIO GELATO: see recipe on
  p. 80.

1. GELATO: prepare the pistachio gelato as indicated on p. 80. Put it aside in the freezer. Fifteen minutes before serving dessert, take it out of the freezer and leave it at room temperature so it softens slightly.

2. AMARETTI (prepare the dough the day before, if possible): in a mixing bowl, combine the slivered almonds and the almond powder, flour, and powdered sugar. Separately, whisk the egg whites until stiff, then incorporate into it the preceding mixture with the pistachio paste. Again, combine with a wooden spoon to get a uniform and rather thick dough. Cover the baking sheet with a leaf of parchment paper. Lay on top small balls of about ⅛ cup of amaretti dough, rolled beforehand on some powdered sugar. Preheat the oven to 300°F, garnish each amaretto with a pistachio nut, put in the oven for 20 minutes.

3. PRESENTATION: on plates left for 1 good hour in the freezer, offer 1 or 2 tablespoons of pistachio gelato, lay on the side 1 or 2 amaretti as they come out of the oven. Garnish with a few caramelized pistachios (p. 204) and some amaretti crumbs coarsely crushed. Serve immediately.

HAZELNUT GELATO WAFFLE WITH CARAMELIZED FIGS

Waffles, crunchy and hot, are an excellent support for gelati. Easy to make, they delight the young and old alike. Here, you top them with a hazelnut gelato.

Difficulty: easy.
Serves: about 6 people
Preparation time: 30 minutes
Setting time: 1 hour
Cooking time: 20 minutes

SPECIAL EQUIPMENT:
12-inch frying pan
waffle iron

INGREDIENTS:
WAFFLES AND GELATO:
2¼ cups flour
⅛ cup sugar
2 tsp baking powder
2 eggs
1½ cups milk
50 g melted butter
Piedmont hazelnut gelato (p. 58)

FRUITS AND FINISHING TOUCHES:
6 nice figs
2 pats butter
4 tbsp honey
3 tbsp Amaretto
chocolate sauce (p. 214)
caramelized hazelnuts (p. 204)
dark chocolate (70 percent or
   more cacao)

1. WAFFLE BATTER: in a mixing bowl, combine the flour, sugar, and baking powder. Add the eggs and half of the milk. Combine well, with a whisk, to get rid of all the lumps. Add the rest of the milk and the melted butter (not too hot). Put aside for 1 hour.

2. FRUITS: cut the figs in two lengthwise. In a large frying pan, let the butter foam at medium heat. Add the figs, pan-fry for 1 or 2 minutes, then place them on a plate. Pour the honey into a hot frying pan, bring to a boil. When it begins to caramelize, add the figs and the Amaretto. Combine gently, remove the frying pan from the heat.

3. PRESENTATION: Cook one waffle, then place it, piping hot, on a plate. Lay on top some chocolate sauce, then two fig halves. Then add the hazelnut gelato and top with a few caramelized hazelnuts. Finish with a few dark chocolate chips, then serve immediately. Then prepare the other waffles, little by little. Forget about preparing the waffles in advance: this method would undoubtedly be more practical, but the result a lot worse . . .

For a little variety
In the summer months, replace the figs with apricots, peaches, or some other fruit in season . . . In winter, consider mango or pineapple . . . Add a bit of whipped cream (p. 206) on the fruits. Consider Amorino tapioca pearls for the garnish.

FOCACCIA (ITALIAN FLAT BREAD) WITH CARAMEL GELATO

Focaccia is a salted specialty and can be wonderfully paired with gelati. For optimal results, it's important to prepare the dough the day before: that way, the focaccia will be a lot more flavorful.

Difficulty: intermediate
Serves: about 6 people
Preparation time: 40 minutes
Setting time: overnight + 3 hours
Cooking time: 20 to 25 minutes

SPECIAL EQUIPMENT:
food processor
parchment paper
electric beater

INGREDIENTS:
FOCACCIA:
⅓ cup powdered sugar
⅗ tsp fine salt
⅛ cup baker's yeast
⅔ cup milk
3 eggs
4 cups flour
⅓ cup cold butter
powdered sugar
slivered almonds

OTHER COMPONENTS:
caramel gelato with salted butter
(p. 50)
whipped cream (p. 206)
caramel sauce (p. 216)

1. FOCACCIA: in a bowl, add the sugar, salt, baker's yeast, milk, and 2 eggs. Combine it all with a hand whisk for a few moments. In the bowl of the electric beater, add the preceding mixture to the flour. Knead at medium speed for 7 to 8 minutes. Add the cold butter cut into little dices, knead again for 3 to 4 minutes, or whatever time is needed for the butter to be fully integrated. Let the dough rest overnight in the fridge.

2. The next day, spread the dough into a rectangle of 50 x 30 cm, more or less. Cut up circles of 7 to 8 cm with a glass. Place the circles on a sheet covered with floured parchment paper and let it rise for 2 to 3 hours. Beat the remaining egg briefly. With a brush, glaze the focaccia, dust them with a little powdered sugar, then sprinkle them with almonds. Let them bake for 20 to 25 minutes in the oven preheated at 325°F. Take them out of the oven, let them cool a bit.

3. PRESENTATION: cut up the focaccia in two and lay them on plates. Place, on the side, some caramel gelato, top with whipped cream and caramel sauce.

Gorgeous . . . and good, too!
You can top your focaccia plates with caramelized nuts (p. 204) or caramel bits (p. 212).

MONT BLANC CUP

Chestnut cream lets you prepare a gelato that's very original and simple to pull off. Churn it at the last moment, so that it's as supple and smooth as it is irresistible.

Difficulty: easy
Serves: about 6 people
Preparation time: 1 hour
Cooking time: 1 minute

INGREDIENTS:
CHESTNUT GELATO:
3 cups milk
⅓ cup heavy cream
1 egg yolk
⅛ cup powdered milk
½ cup powdered sugar
1 cup chestnut cream
3 tbsp Armagnac (optional; or chestnut gelato, p. 72)

OTHER COMPONENTS:
Chantilly or whipped cream
   (p. 206)
3 oz glazed chestnut chips
a few Amorino "ossi di morti"
   ("bones of the dead") cookies

1. GELATO: in a mixer, add the cold milk, heavy cream, egg yolk, powdered milk, and sugar. Blend for a few moments. If you don't own a mixer, whisk these ingredients by hand in a mixing bowl.

2. Pour the contents into a saucepan. Heat, stirring constantly with a whisk. When the contents just begins to simmer (at a temperature of 185°F, if you own a thermometer), take the saucepan off the heat and let cool thoroughly. Then add the chestnut cream and the Armagnac, if you decide to use it. Pour the contents into an ice cream maker and let it set. When the gelato is set, place it in a storage container in the freezer.

3. PRESENTATION: in well-chilled glasses, serve some chestnut gelato. Top with whipped cream, sprinkle with glazed chestnuts and a few crumbs of coarsely crushed Amorino "ossi di morti" cookies.

For a little variety
Offer this recipe in dessert shells (p. 182).

ZEPPOLE, AMARETTO ZABAGLIONE, AND DARK CHOCOLATE GELATO

Zeppole are deep-fried doughnuts. Here, they are served still hot with an amoretto zabaglione and dark chocolate gelato, in a very epicurean version.

Difficulty: intermediate
Serves: about 6 people
Preparation time: 30 minutes
Setting time: overnight + 3 hours
Cooking time: 5 minutes

SPECIAL EQUIPMENT:
food processor
parchment paper

INGREDIENTS:
AMARETTO ZABAGLIONE: See recipe on p. 222, replace cold water with Amaretto
DARK CHOCOLATE GELATO: See recipe on p. 52

ZEPPOLE:
⅓ cup powdered sugar
¾ tsp fine salt
⅙ cup baker's yeast
¾ cup milk, 2 eggs
3⅓ cups flour
⅓ cup cold butter

COOKING AND GARNISH:
1 quart cooking oil (peanut, sunflower)
powdered sugar
a few caramelized almonds (p. 204)

1. ZEPPOIE: in a bowl, add the sugar, salt, baker's yeast, milk, and eggs. Combine it all with a hand whisk for a few moments.

2. In the bowl of the electric mixer, add the preceding mixture to the flour. Knead at medium speed for 7 to 8 minutes. Add the cold butter cut into little dices, knead again for 3 to 4 minutes, or whatever time is needed for the butter to be fully integrated. Let the dough rest overnight in the fridge.

3. The next day, spread the dough into a rectangle of 12 x 20 inches, more or less. Cut up circles of 3 to 3½ inches with a glass. Place the circles on a sheet covered with floured parchment paper and let it rise for 2 to 3 hours. Heat the oil in a frying pan (not more than 550°F, if you have a thermometer). Fry the zeppole for 4 to 5 minutes, turning them. Drain them, pat them dry on a paper towel. Sprinkle them with powdered sugar.

4. ZABAGLIONE AND CHOCOLATE GELATO: prepare these recipes as indicated on pp. 222 and 52.

5. PRESENTATION: with a serrated knife, open up the warm zeppole, as you would do with a hamburger bun. Very quickly, lay 1 or 2 tablespoons of zabaglione on one of the zeppole halves. Immediately add the chocolate gelato, a bit, a lot, or passionately . . . Top with a few caramelized almonds. Lay the zeppole on plates, place on top or on the side their "hats," sprinkle a bit of sugar and serve without delay.

Quick tip
The recipe listed here will give you more zeppole than you need . . . Eat those that are left over as is, or with a little Chantilly cream (p. 206), some melted chocolate . . . You can also make this recipe by fashioning some "mini" zeppole . . .

STRAWBERRY, LEMON, AND PASSION FRUIT NAPOLEON

Here's how to transform, simply, succulent sorbets into a spectacular dessert. Once you acquire the simple preparation technique, you'll be able to vary this recipe endlessly.

Difficulty: intermediate
Serves: 6 to 8 people
Preparation time: 40 minutes
Time in freezer: 3 hours

SPECIAL EQUIPMENT:
rectangular mold at least 3 ½ in high

INGREDIENTS:
strawberry sorbet (p. 96)
lemon sorbet (p. 94)
passion fruit sorbet (p. 92)
raspberry coulis (p. 210)
mango coulis (p. 210)
¾ cup red berries (strawberries, raspberries, black currant berries, red currants, etc.)
a few mint leaves

1. Place the rectangular mold in the freezer for a good half hour to ice it. Conversely, take out the strawberry sorbet from the freezer to soften it a bit.

2. Lay some strawberry sorbet at the bottom of the mold. Without putting any on the walls, spread it to get a layer of at least 1 inch. Level and smooth the surface, with the back of a tablespoon soaked in warm water.

3. Place the mold in the freezer for at least 1 hour. Now remove the lemon sorbet from the freezer (for 20 to 25 minutes). Stir it in its storage container, with a spoon, to make it malleable. Lay a 1-inch layer of lemon sorbet on the strawberry sorbet, spread, smooth the surface. Put back in the freezer for 1 hour. Finish it with a layer of passion fruit sorbet, let harden for another hour.

4. PRESENTATION: Remove the sorbet napoleon by soaking the mold 1 or 2 seconds in warm water, cut it up into slices. Serve the slices on cold plates with a little strawberry and mango coulis. Garnish with red berries and mint. Serve without delay.

For a little variety
Between the layers of the sorbets, slip a thin layer of melted dark chocolate, spread with a brush. Or maybe arrange some thin mint leaves . . . Replace the sorbets with gelati, to your liking. Pair, for instance, with spice cookie, coffee, and chocolate gelato.

CHOCOLATE CAKE WITH VANILLA AND CHOCOLATE GELATO

Chocolate "torta" (cake) is an Italian sweet that's especially delicious when served with vanilla gelato. Ideally, offer it while it's still a little warm.

Difficulty: easy
Serves: 6 to 8 people
Preparation time: 40 minutes
Cooking time: 25 to 30 minutes

SPECIAL EQUIPMENT:
round cake pan (2 inches tall and 10 inches diameter)
electric beater

INGREDIENTS:
CAKE: 7 oz dark chocolate
  (75 percent cacao)
½ cup butter + some for mold
4 eggs
1½ cups powdered sugar
1 teaspoon cornstarch
1 pinch salt

OTHER COMPONENTS:
bourbon vanilla gelato (p. 66)
1¾ oz dark chocolate
chocolate and vanilla sauces
  (pp. 214 and 202)
Chantilly cream (p. 206)

1. CAKE: in a not-too-hot double boiler, melt the dark chocolate with the butter. Separately, preheat the oven to 350°F. Separate the egg whites from the yolks.

2. In a mixing bowl, whisk the yolks for about 30 seconds with 1 cup of powdered sugar, then add the cornstarch. In another mixing bowl, beat the white to a very firm peak with the salt. Add the remaining powdered sugar, beat another moment.

3. Add the chocolate and the butter to the mixture containing the egg yolks. Then, gently incorporate into the whipped whites. Pour the dough into the buttered round cake pan, put it in the oven, let bake for 25 to 30 minutes. Remove the cake from the oven, then take it out of the mold and place onto a serving plate.

4. PRESENTATION: serve the cake to your liking: cut it into portions, offer it in a plate with gelato, a little sauce, and Chantilly cream.

Good . . . and gorgeous, too!
Bake the cake dough in little round individual molds. Pour the chocolate and vanilla sauces onto plates, to achieve beautiful color contrasts. Place the gelato on the sauce, add the cake cut in two, top with a little Chantilly cream.

"RAFFAELLO" COCONUT CUP

The "Raffaello" is a confection extremely appreciated in Italy and prepared at home. You eat it without fuss, at all hours, but you can also enjoy it for dessert, with, for instance, a nice coconut gelato.

Difficulty: intermediate
Serves: 6 to 8 people
Preparation time: 40 minutes
Setting time: 2 hours

INGREDIENTS:
RAFFAELLO MORSELS:
7 oz white chocolate
½ cup light cream
¾ cup powdered coconut + some
  for coating of morsels
whole shelled unsalted almonds

OTHER COMPONENTS:
3 oz white chocolate
coconut gelato (p. 70)
Amorino tapioca pearls

1. MORSELS: finely chop or grate the 7 oz white chocolate. In a small saucepan, boil the cream, remove it from the heat, add the chocolate. Combine to get a uniform mass. Add the coconut, combine. Place the contents in a container and let it cool and harden a bit in the fridge for about 2 hours.

2. With your hands, set some chocolate paste aside, bury an almond inside, and form a ball. Roll it into the coconut, place it on a plate, keep it in the fridge.

3. CHOCOLATE: melt the 3 oz white chocolate in the double boiler.

4. PRESENTATION: lay a bit of white chocolate on the bottom of the cups, then a nice scoop or petal of coconut gelato and the Tapioca pearls. Serve with the morsels.

For a little variety
For a more colorful presentation, also prepare some morsels with dark chocolate, putting, inside, some whole caramelized hazelnuts (p. 204).

TIRAMISU PLATE

Dive into the very heart of the best of Italian tradition with this epicurean and generous dessert. Ideally, prepare the tiramisu the day before.

Difficulty: intermediate
Serves: about 6 people
Preparation time: 1 hour
Setting time: a few hours
Time in freezer: at least 1 hour

SPECIAL EQUIPMENT:
espresso maker
electric beater

INGREDIENTS:
TIRAMISU:
6 espressos (Sidamo, if possible)
4 egg yolks
¾ cups powdered sugar
⅔ cup light cream
¼ cup powdered sugar
1½ cups mascarpone
4 tbsp Amaretto
6 ladyfingers
a few Amorino
Amarena cherries
powdered bitter cocoa

GELATO:
fior di latte gelato (p. 68)
1 tbsp coffee extract
powdered bitter cocoa

1. TIRAMISU: prepare the espressos. Pour them into a soup plate. Let cool. Place the egg yolks and the powdered sugar in a mixing bowl, barely simmering on a double boiler, then beat it all on high for about 7 to 8 minutes. Take the mixing bowl off the double boiler, beat another 5 minutes at medium, put aside. Separately, beat the light cream and the powdered sugar firmly. In a third mixing bowl, gently stir (for a short time) the mascarpone to soften it; add the whipped cream, the yolks, and the Amaretto. Gently combine for the least time possible.

2. Soak a ladyfinger for a few moments in the coffee, cut it in two. On the bottom of a glass, lay half a ladyfinger with coffee, 1 or 2 cherries, then, on top, the tiramisu contents. Lay on the second half of the ladyfinger and 1 or 2 cherries. Cover with the tiramisu contents. Sprinkle with bitter cocoa, to your liking. Cover with plastic wrap, let rest in a cool place for a few hours.

3. GELATO: prepare the gelato as indicated on p. 68, adding to it the coffee extract. The moment you take it out of the ice cream maker, proceed as follows: lay a layer of gelato about ¾ or 1¼ inches thick in a storage container. With a fine strainer, sprinkle some bitter cocoa.

Lay on top another layer of gelato of about the same thickness, sprinkle some cocoa again, and so on, until there's no more gelato. Finish it with a layer of cocoa. Let set in the freezer for at least 1 hour.

4. PRESENTATION: offer the tiramisus in their glasses. Take the storage container of gelato out of the freezer, take some gelato with a tablespoon, and serve it, also in a glass. Top with one or two Amorino Amarena cherries.

For a little variety
More difficult and more refined: you can also take the block of gelato out of the mold and cut it into slices, with a knife soaked in warm water.

SEMIFREDDO WITH BOURBON VANILLA

There exists not one, not ten, not a hundred, but thousands of recipes of semifreddo (semi-frozen desserts): with fruits, without fruits, with cream or without. Here's a version of it that you'll enjoy garnishing with superb little Amorino tapioca pearls.

Difficulty: intermediate
Serves: about 6 people
Preparation time: 40 minutes
Time in freezer: at least 5 hours 30 minutes

SPECIAL EQUIPMENT:
electric beater
candy thermometer
rectangular mold
pastry bag
(optional)

INGREDIENTS:
SEMIFREDDO:
3 bourbon vanilla beans
6 egg yolks
1 cup powdered sugar
¼ cup cold water
⅚ cup cold light cream

OTHER COMPONENTS:
strawberry sorbet (p. 86)
Chantilly cream (p. 206)
Amorino tapioca pearls

1. VANILLA SEMIFREDDO: with a small knife, split the vanilla beans in two lengthwise and scrape the half-beans to collect the little black seeds within. Beat the yolks with the vanilla seeds at medium so that they blanch and, little by little, swell and enlarge. Place the rectangular mold in the freezer.

2. At this point, add the sugar, empty vanilla half-beans, and water in a saucepan. Bring to a boil. When the syrup reaches a temperature of 225 to 230°F, remove the saucepan from the heat and pour the red-hot syrup (without the half-beans) on the well-beaten yolks (and, above all, beating them constantly!). Set the beater at its highest setting, then let cool for 5 minutes. Continue to cool, now beating the zabaglione at medium/low for 5 more minutes.

3. Separately, beat the very cold light cream firmly. Combine the zabaglione with the light cream.

4. ASSEMBLING THE DESSERT: in the rectangular mold, pour half of the vanilla semifreddo. Place in the freezer, let solidify for 2 hours. Then add a layer of strawberry sorbet, then pour the rest of the vanilla semifreddo contents on top. Place in the freezer for at least 3 hours.

5. PRESENTATION: remove the semifreddo from the mold, place it on a long chilled plate. With a pastry bag, or a spoon and a spatula, cloak all of it with Chantilly cream. Place the semifreddo in the freezer for a half hour to solidify the Chantilly cream a bit. Next, garnish it in the most whimsical way possible with Amorino tapioca pearls. Serve immediately, cut up in slices with a knife soaked in warm water.

LEMON CUP WITH LIMONCELLO

Limoncello is a highly valued alcoholic drink in Italy. Here, it is used to underline the refined flavor of a lemon sorbet served in a jewelry case of pastry.

Difficulty: difficult
Serves: about 6 people
Preparation time: 1 hour
Setting time: 2 hours
Cooking time: a few minutes

SPECIAL EQUIPMENT:
parchment paper
pastry bag

INGREDIENTS:
DESSERT SHELLS:
3 to 4 egg whites
½ cup butter
1 vanilla bean
1 cup powdered sugar
1 cup flour

LEMON CREAM:
¼ cup butter, cut into pieces
3 egg yolks
¾ cup water
¾ cup lemon juice
¾ cup powdered sugar
⅛ cup cornstarch

OTHER COMPONENTS:
lemon sorbet (p. 94)
limoncello
Amorino tapioca pearls

1. DESSERT SHELLS: leave the egg whites at room temperature. Also, take out the butter from the fridge, let it soften thoroughly. It should take on the consistency of face cream. Cut the vanilla bean in two lengthwise. With a small knife, scrape the insides of the half-beans to collect the little black seeds within.

2. In a mixing bowl, combine the soft butter with the vanilla seeds and the powdered sugar. Add the egg whites, little by little, and combine continually. Last, add the flour. Combine again. Let the dough rest in the fridge for 2 hours.

3. Preheat the oven to 350°F. Cover the baking sheet with parchment paper. Mix up the dough to soften it. Lay 6 nice clumps of dough, with lots of space between. Spread them with a spatula to make circles of about 2¾ to 3¼ inches in diameter. Put them in the oven for 8 to 10 minutes. Remove the dough circles from the oven, unstick them, place them in bowls or cups, fitting them exactly, let them cool.

4. LEMON CREAM : in a saucepan, combine all the ingredients for the cream. Heat on medium, combining continually with a whisk. When the preparation thickens and begins to boil, remove the saucepan from the heat, pour the cream into a mixing bowl, and put aside.

5. PRESENTATION: place the dessert shells on plates. With a pastry bag, lay some lemon cream on the bottom of the shells. Lay on top some lemon sorbet. Baste with limoncello, top with a few Amorino tapioca pearls, serve immediately, before the delicate pastry of the shell softens.

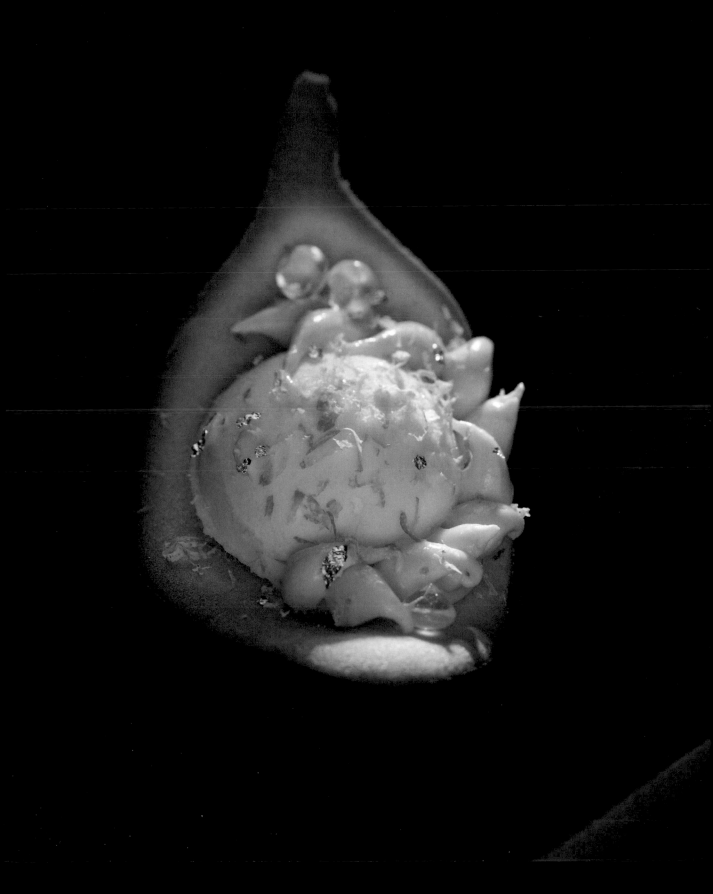

PANNA COTTA, PANNA COTTA GELATO, CARAMEL, AND FRUITS

Panna cotta is also eaten in the form of gelato. Paired with a few fruits and a delectable caramel sauce, it earns universal approval.

Difficulty: difficult
Serves: about 6 people
Preparation time: 50 minutes
Cooking time: 20 minutes
Time in freezer: 6 hours

INGREDIENTS:
PANNA COTTA: 6 edible gelatin
  leaves
3½ cups light cream
1 cup milk
1½ cups powdered sugar

OTHER COMPONENTS:
cream gelato (p. 54)
cold caramel sauce (p. 216)
3 pears in syrup (p. 34)
bitter cocoa
6 figs
a few red and white grapes
1 pat butter
Chantilly cream (p. 206)

1. PANNA COTTA: soak the gelatin leaves in cold water. In a saucepan, add the milk, light cream, and the sugar, then heat on low, stirring regularly, for 15 minutes (being careful not to boil the contents). Away from the heat, add the dried gelatin leaves (be sure they are melted completely). Then pour the contents (after straining it with a strainer) into a mixing bowl or 6 small ramekins. Cover with plastic wrap and let set in the fridge for 12 hours.

2. GELATO: prepare the cream gelato (p. 54), then fill the storage container with one-third of the gelato. Smooth the surface, lay on top a layer of not-too-thick and very cold caramel sauce. (Ideally, let each caramel layer solidify in the freezer before covering with gelato.) Cover with gelato (another third), cover with caramel sauce, then cover with the final third of gelato and finish it with a thin layer of caramel sauce. Place the prepared storage container in the freezer for about 6 hours.

3. FRUITS: drain the pears, cut them to your liking. Cut up the figs in quarters. Peel the grapes. Sauté the fruits for a few moments in the foaming butter.

4. PRESENTATION: if the panna cotta is in a mixing bowl, take a tablespoon of it and lay it on a plate. Sprinkle a fine trace of bitter cocoa. In perfect harmony, surround the panna cotta with the fruits. Lay on the side, on the caramel, 1 or 2 tablespoons of panna cotta gelato. Top the plate with a bit of caramel sauce and Chantilly cream. If the panna cotta is prepared in ramekins, top it with cocoa and serve it on the side.

For a little variety
Instead of creating layers of caramel sauce as indicated above, consider other preparations like strawberry, raspberry, and mango coulis (p. 210) or candied orange sauce (p. 220). In any case, this layer of sauce shouldn't be more than ⅛ inch thick.

DARK CHOCOLATE AFFOGATO

Simplicity is often the secret even of the best recipes. Here, the very natural union of coffee and dark chocolate gives life and solace to this irresistible specialty.

Difficulty: easy
Serves: 2 people
Preparation time: 2 minutes

SPECIAL EQUIPMENT:
espresso maker

INGREDIENTS:
dark chocolate gelato (p. 52)
2 espressos containing ⅔ to 1 cup
  Sidamo coffee
powdered bitter cocoa

1. Place 2 serving cups in the freezer. Take the chocolate gelato out of the freezer.

2. With 2 tablespoons, lay 2 nice petals, scoops, or spoonfuls of chocolate gelato in the very cold cups.

3. Fill the percolator with Sidamo coffee and pour it, with its flavorful foam, directly on the chocolate gelato. Sprinkle with a tiny mist of bitter cocoa. Eat immediately to make the most of the unique "hot-cold" effect of this recipe.

Quick tip
In order to lay only a tiny quantity of cocoa on this dessert, begin by crumbling (if you need to) the bitter cocoa with a fork. Then place 1 teaspoon of it in a very fine strainer. Tap the strainer very gently with the handle of a spoon above the coffee.

STRAWBERRY ZUPPA INGLESE

Every Italian family has its own recipe for zuppa inglese. So here's a version of it that you'll enjoy personalizing by changing the gelati, the fruits, the sauce, etc.

Difficulty: easy
Serves: about 6 people
Preparation time: 20 minutes
Cooking time: 10 minutes

INGREDIENTS:
vanilla sauce (p. 202)
strawberry sorbet (p. 96)
1 lb strawberries
½ cup sugar syrup
½ cup Amaretto
½ cup cold water
a few ladyfingers
Chantilly cream (p. 206)
Caramelized nuts (optional for
  garnish, see p. 204)
Amorino tapioca pearls (optional
  for garnish)

1. If possible, prepare the vanilla sauce the day before and store in the fridge so it's very cold the day you prepare this dessert. The same day, make the strawberry sorbet as indicated on p. 96.

2. Wash the strawberries, remove the stems, then cut them in two lengthwise. Place the syrup in a soup bowl, add the Amaretto and the cold water to it, combine.

3. Place 6 very cold bowls or cups or soup bowls in front of you. Depending on the size of the bowls or cups, soak 1 or 2, or even 3 ladyfingers for a few moments in the syrup, then place them in a plate, in the center. On the side, pour some vanilla sauce, a little or a lot, to your liking. Lay on top 1 or 2 nice scoops of strawberry sorbet. Top it all with the strawberries and a little Chantilly cream. You can finish off the garnish by adding a few caramelized nuts (p. 204) or, better still, some Amorino tapioca pearls. Serve very cool, without delay.

For a little variety
Why not replace the vanilla sauce with a succulent mango coulis (p. 210)?

CHOCOLATE CHIP GELATO SANDWICH

Discover this Italian specialty that all kids know. Parents also, from memory or pure gustatory joy, gladly eat these frozen vanilla sandwiches.

Difficulty: easy
Serves: about 6 people
Preparation time: 20 minutes
Cooking time: none
Time in freezer: 1 or 2 hours

INGREDIENTS:
12 butter cookies
chocolate chip gelato (p. 64)
your choice of chocolate or
   vanilla sauce (pp. 214 and 202;
   optional)
Chantilly cream (p. 206; optional).

1. Place the butter cookies in the freezer for a good half hour to freeze them thoroughly. Conversely, take the chocolate chip gelato out of the freezer so that it softens and is more malleable.

2. Take a generous tablespoon of chocolate chip gelato, place it on a frozen cookie and spread it to obtain a layer that is rather flat and 1 to 1½ inches thick. Place a cookie on the gelato to form a sandwich. Level the gelato "sides" all around the sandwiches, to make them flat and even. Place the sandwiches in the freezer and let them harden a bit, for at least 1 hour.

3. In general, kids eat these sandwiches holding them in their hands, with little fuss, but you can also offer them in plates with a bit of chocolate (or vanilla) sauce and a little Chantilly cream.

For a little variety
Replace the chocolate chip gelato with another gelato of your choice or, even more daring, with a sorbet. You can also prepare more complex sandwiches with 2 layers of gelati or sorbets of different colors. And even better, insert some fruits and some chocolate shavings between the layers of gelato.

PANETTONE WITH CHANTILLY CREAM AND CARAMELIZED PISTACHIOS

In Italy, panettone is everywhere. Every family has its own recipe, but they are all presented in the same way: a cylinder, bulging and golden brown. Served warm and toasted with a caramel salted-butter gelato.

Difficulty: intermediate
Serves: 6 to 8 people
Preparation time: 1 hour
Setting time: overnight + 1 hour 30 minutes
Cooking time: 25 to 30 minutes.

SPECIAL EQUIPMENT:
electric kneading machine
panettone mold

INGREDIENTS:
PANETTONE:
⅙ cup raisins
½ cup Amaretto
1 cup butter + some for mold
5 eggs
⅛ cup baker's yeast
⅙ cup milk
3⅓ cups flour + some for mold
½ tbsp salt
¼ cup powdered sugar
3 oz candied orange and lemon
  zests, cut in two

OTHER COMPONENTS:
Chantilly cream (p. 206)
caramel gelato with salted butter
caramelized pistachios (p. 204)

1. PANETTONE: the day before, soak the raisins in the Amaretto. Take the butter out of the fridge so it softens. Break the eggs, beat them lightly. Pour them into the bowl of the kneading machine (put a small amount of it aside). Add the baker's yeast, milk, flour, salt, and sugar. Knead these ingredients for 10 minutes on medium. While you are kneading, add the juice from the raisins. Add the butter cut into small pieces. When the butter is incorporated, add the raisins and the zests. Combine gently so as not to bruise them. Put the dough in the fridge overnight.

2. BAKING OF THE PANETTONE: the next day, work the very cold dough, form a ball (or two, depending on the size of the one or more molds). Butter the mold, flour it, then slip the dough in it. Let the panettone swell for an hour and a half. Preheat the oven to 325°F. Brown the surface of the panettone with some of the leftover beaten eggs, put in the oven, and bake for 25 to 30 minutes or a bit more, depending on the mold. Take the panettone out of the oven, remove it from the mold, let it cool.

3. PRESENTATION: cut the panettone into not-too-thin slices. Toast them in a toaster. Lay them on plates. At the very last moment, lay the Chantilly cream on top, then a petal of caramel gelato. Garnish with a few caramelized pistachios, serve immediately.

Good . . . and gorgeous, too!
Pair this dessert with a chocolate sauce (p. 214).

For a little variety
Replace the Chantilly cream with a chocolate or praline whipped cream (p. 206).

PEAR AND CHOCOLATE CUP WITH HOMEMADE BISCUITS

The classic combination of chocolate and pear never disappoints. This delicious dessert is quick and easy to make.

Difficulty: intermediate
Serves: about 6 people
Preparation time: 20 minutes
Setting time: 2 hours
Cooking time: about 10 minutes

INGREDIENTS:
WAFERS:
3 to 4 egg whites
½ cup butter + 1 tsp for the sheet
1 vanilla bean
1 cup powdered sugar
1 cup flour
slivered almonds

CUPS:
6 pears cooked in syrup (p. 34)
bourbon vanilla gelato (p. 66)
chocolate sauce (p. 214)
a few caramelized pistachios
  (p. 204)

1. WAFERS: leave the egg whites at room temperature. Take the butter out of the fridge, let it soften completely. It should be the consistency of face cream. Cut the vanilla bean in two lengthwise, scrape the insides of the half-beans to collect the little black seeds within.

2. In a mixing bowl, combine the soft butter with the vanilla seeds and the powdered sugar. Add the whites, little by little, combining continually. Last, add, the flour. Combine again. Let the dough rest in the fridge for 2 hours.

3. Preheat the oven at 325°F. Butter the baking sheet, lay on it some dough knobs, with space in between. Spread them out in circles. Sprinkle them with slivered almonds. Put in the oven for about ten minutes. Take the wafers out of the oven, unstick them, and let them cool.

4. EASY PRESENTATION: in well-chilled cups, lay the cooked pears, whole or cut, to your liking. Lay some vanilla gelato on top, coat with a little chocolate sauce, sprinkle with pistachios, serve immediately with the wafers on the side.

5. MORE DIFFICULT PRESENTATION, AS NAPOLEON: place the wafers in the freezer. Slice a few pears, place them also in the freezer. Place the vanilla gelato in a pastry bag, put it in the freezer. On the plates, place a wafer. Cover with 1 or 2 pear slices, lay some gelato on top, sprinkle with a few pistachios. Place a wafer on top, repeat the process until you place 3 or 4 wafers total. Serve with chocolate sauce.

For a little variety
Even better, offer these pears in dessert shells (p. 182).

SAUCES AND SIDE DISHES

- Vanilla, caramel, chocolate, red berries . . . -

Don't settle for simplicity

*A scoop of strawberry sorbet or of
vanilla gelato is always enough just by itself. But the temptation
to do even better is always in the back of your mind . . .*

So, the same scoop of vanilla gelato accompanied by a hot chocolate sauce, a little whipped cream, a wafer, or a waffle can take on a whole new flavor . . . Here, everything resides in the art of pairing, which, always, must remain balanced and harmonious. Thus, a side dish, whatever it is, must never overshadow what it is supposed to garnish. It has to do with ornamenting, embellishing, enriching, enhancing a gelato or a sorbet, never to mask or alter it. It's why good taste, economy, and restraint must always take precedence in this matter. A side dish is actually what it is: a simple improvement to accompany but not overshadow your dessert; the gelato or the sorbet have to remain the undeniable stars.

VANILLA SAUCE

Vanilla sauce is an unavoidable element in side dishes for gelati. It is easy to make, and better if you prepare it the day before. To pull it off, there's only one solution: use lots of very good vanilla.

Difficulty: easy
Serves: about 6 people
Preparation time: 30 minutes
Cooking time: 20 minutes
Setting time: 30 minutes

INGREDIENTS:
2 cups milk
¼ cup light cream
2 bourbon vanilla beans
3 egg yolks
⅓ cup powdered sugar
¹⁄₁₆ cup cornstarch

1. In a saucepan, add the milk and cream. Cut the vanilla beans in two lengthwise. With the point of a knife, scrape the insides of the half-beans to collect the pulp within. Add the cut beans and the pulp to the milk-cream mixture. Give it a little whisk. Heat, then bring the milk to a simmer. Cover the saucepan, remove it from the heat, and let infuse for 30 minutes.

2. During this time, combine the egg yolks and the sugar in a mixing bowl with a whisk. Add the cornstarch, combine. Pour the milk with the vanilla on top. Combine thoroughly. Pour this mixture back into the saucepan and heat on low, combining continually for about 7 to 8 minutes. When the sauce thickens (at a temperature of 185°F,

if you have a thermometer), remove the saucepan from the heat. Filter the sauce at once through a fine strainer, let cool thoroughly. Pour the vanilla sauce in a hermetically sealed container and place it immediately in the fridge until ready for use. Don't keep it for more than 2 days.

For a little variety
Vanilla sauce is truly "all-purpose," provided, of course, that you serve it very cold, almost frozen. It can be happily paired with gelato (especially vanilla, cream, and mascarpone), as well as sorbets (strawberry, naturally), but also various creations: zeppole, semifreddo, cookies, panettone, etc.

CARAMELIZED NUTS

Caramelized nuts are unavoidable: delicious and very appetizing, they bring, every time, a note of refinement. What's more, their crunchy texture creates a pleasant contrast with the smoothness and creaminess of gelati and sorbets.

Difficulty: easy
Serves: about 6 people
Preparation time: 5 minutes
Cooking time: 10 to 15 minutes

SPECIAL EQUIPMENT:
large 12-inch frying pan
parchment paper

INGREDIENTS:
5 oz nuts
½ cup powdered sugar
1 tsp powdered glucose (p. 26: this will facilitate the recipe, but it's not indispensable)

1. Place the frying pan on low heat. Add the nuts, sugar, and glucose powder, if you are using it. Combine with a wooden spoon. After 3 or 4 minutes, the sugar will begin to melt. At this point, combine well to coat the nuts. Continue cooking, combining continually (be aware of the edges of the pan where the nuts tend to brown too much).

2. When the caramel is gold, dark gold, brown, or dark brown, depending on the cooking time you have given it, pour the nuts onto a sheet of parchment paper. Spread them with the wooden spoon to separate and to best differentiate them. Let cool. Then place the caramelized nuts in a hermetically sealed box and use them rather quickly (in the next 2 or 3 days).

Possible nuts (or seeds)
Almonds, hazelnuts, pistachios, cashews, pecans all work. You can also use sesame seeds . . . Additionally, you can vary the flavor and look of your caramelized nuts by replacing the powdered sugar with brown sugar, Muscovado sugar, honey, etc.

Tip
The use of caramelized nuts on gelati is nearly universal. You can also sprinkle them either whole or chopped, as finely as you'd like. They can also be incorporated directly in gelati, at the end of the mixing process. Don't prepare the nuts too far in advance (no more than 2 or 3 days), since the caramel that covers them ends up softening and melting.

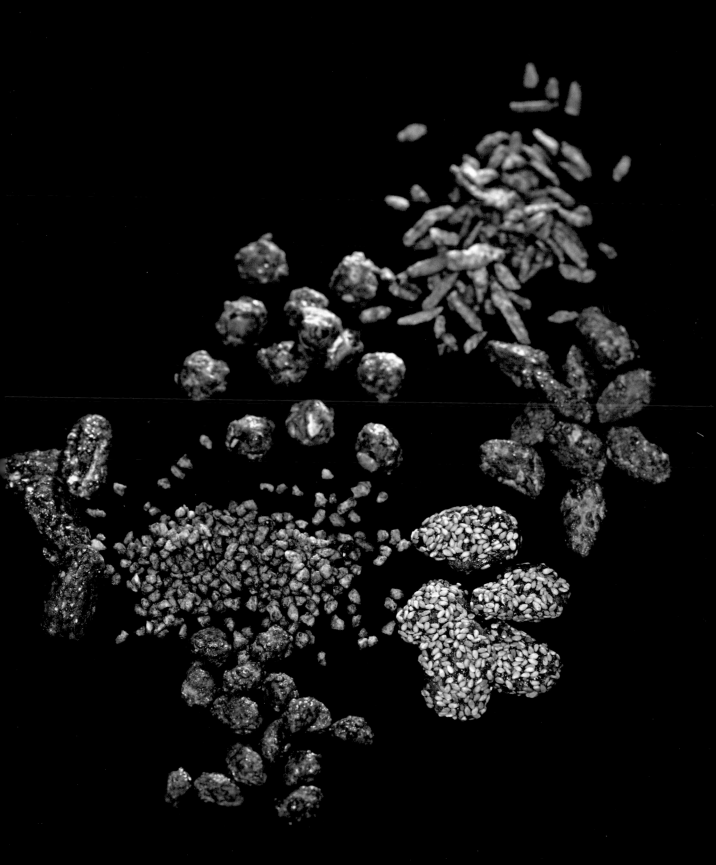

WHIPPED CREAMS, PLAIN AND FLAVORED

Whipped creams, which are easy to make, have the greatest impact on gelati, sorbets, and other creations. Chantilly cream is of course the best known, but other delicious and more creative variations exist.

Difficulty: easy.
Serves: 4 to 6 people.

SPECIAL EQUIPMENT:
electric beater
a whipping siphon (optional)

INGREDIENTS:
1 cup light cream (at least 30 percent fat)
¼ cup powdered sugar

Plain whipped cream

Add the cold cream and sugar in a cold mixing bowl, beat firmly with the electric beater. You can also prepare this recipe by dispensing the whipped cream with a whipping siphon setup.

Many variations are possible. Thanks to them, you can vary your creations endlessly.

VARIATIONS

Vanilla whipped cream
Collect the insides of 2 bourbon vanilla beans, in a mixing bowl combine with 1 cup of cream and ¼ cup of powdered sugar. Whip it or dispense with a whipping siphon.

Chocolate whipped cream
In a saucepan, heat (above all without boiling) 1½ cups of light cream with 1⅓ oz of dark chocolate (at least 70 percent cacao) and ¼ cup of powdered sugar. Combine thoroughly. Let cool, strain, place in the freezer, then, when the cream is chilled, whip it or dispense with a whipping siphon.

Coffee whipped cream
In a mixing bowl, combine with 1 cup of light cream, 1 level teaspoon of freeze-dried coffee, and ¼ cup of powdered sugar. Whip it or dispense with a whipping siphon.

Jasmine tea-flavored whipped cream

In a saucepan, add 1½ cups of light cream and 1 teaspoon of jasmine tea. Heat (without letting boil), then remove the saucepan from the heat. Let infuse for 8 to 10 minutes. Add ¼ cup of powdered sugar. Combine thoroughly. Let cool, place in the freezer, then, when the cream is well chilled, whip it or dispense with a whipping siphon.

Praline whipped cream

In a saucepan, add 1½ cups of light cream and ½ cup of powdered praline. Heat (without letting boil), then remove the saucepan from the heat. Let infuse for 8 to 10 minutes, strain with a very fine strainer. Let cool, place in the freezer, then, when the cream is well chilled, whip it or dispense with a whipping siphon.

Lime whipped cream

In a saucepan, add 1½ cups of light cream and the zest of half an organic lime (without the white skin). Heat (without letting boil), then remove the saucepan from the heat. Cover, let infuse, and cool thoroughly. Strain. Add ¼ cup of powdered sugar. Combine thoroughly. Let cool, place in the freezer, then, when the cream is well chilled, whip it or dispense with a whipping siphon.

Use

Plain or vanilla whipped creams are used almost universally with gelati, sorbets, and other creations. When they are flavored, their marriages must be "arranged." Lime whipped cream is perfect with sorbets made with red berries that are a bit tart, like raspberries, black currants, or strawberries. Praline whipped cream loves gelati with mascarpone, caramel, etc. It's up to you to discover the best "couplings."

FRUIT COULIS

Coulis are rather easy to prepare and bring with them an inimitable refinement. Their fresh and fruity flavor works wonders with gelati as with sorbets. If you own a freezer, prepare them in the summer months and freeze them to enjoy later.

Difficulty: easy
Serves: about 6 people
Preparation time: 20 minutes

SPECIAL EQUIPMENT:
mixer

INGREDIENTS:
STRAWBERRY COULIS:
14 oz strawberries
⅓ cup very cold mineral water
juice of ½ lemon
¼ cup powdered sugar (more or
 less, depending on the fruits)

Wash the strawberries, remove the stems, and cut them in two. Beat them finely with the mineral water, lemon juice, and sugar. Strain the resulting pulp to remove all the seeds; the coulis is ready. Use it right away or freeze it, since it changes very rapidly, losing its delicate flavor.

For a little variety
Try coulis made with raspberries (expect to use more sugar), black currants (expect to use more water), mangoes, pears, yellow peaches cooked in syrup, or passion fruit, etc.

Use the coulis either to coat your gelati and sorbets or to prepare a "bed" in the soup bowls or cups on which to lay your frozen desserts. Perhaps you should avoid pairing coulis that are rather tart (black currant and passion fruit, for instance) with gelati rich in cream (mascarpone, cream), since their flavors are rather conflicting. On the other hand, an assortment of sorbets paired with a nice raspberry coulis is a refined pleasure.

CARAMELS

Caramels bring to your gelati very pleasant notes that are almost spicy. Liquid or brittle, plain or flavored, they always create a pleasant surprise.

Difficulty: difficult
Serves: 4 to 6 people
Preparation time: 20 minutes
Cooking time: 5 to 10 minutes

SPECIAL EQUIPMENT:
parchment paper

INGREDIENTS:
CARAMEL COATING:
3 cups powdered sugar
1 cup water
1 tbsp glucose powder (p. 26)

BRITTLE CARAMEL, CARAMEL SLIVERS:
3 cups powdered sugar
1 cup water
1 tbsp glucose powder (p. 26)

CARAMEL COATING

In a saucepan, add the sugar, half of the water, and glucose powder. Combine, then bring to a boil. Boil the resulting syrup at medium-low, never at high. When the sugar begins to brown, place on low heat. Soak a small piece of parchment paper in the forming caramel, then look at it: you can visualize the ultimate color of your caramel. When the shade of the caramel looks good to you, remove the saucepan from the heat and soak it in a little cold water. Be careful not to burn yourself. Add the rest of the water (watch out for the steam). Combine thoroughly, then let cool.

Use

Use this caramel to top your gelati, coat them, garnish the plates and the cups, or simply to prepare a caramel gelato (in the recipe for cream gelato on p. 54, replace the sugar with liquid caramel).

BRITTLE CARAMEL, CARAMEL SLIVERS

In a saucepan, add the sugar, water, and glucose powder. Combine, then bring to a boil. Boil the resulting syrup at medium-low, never at high. When the sugar begins to brown, place on low heat. Soak a small piece of parchment paper in the forming caramel, then look at it: you can visualize the ultimate color of your caramel. When the shade of the caramel looks good to you, remove the saucepan from the heat and soak it in a little cold water. Be careful not to burn yourself. Pour the caramel on the parchment paper, which has been placed on the baking sheet. Let harden thoroughly. Then break, more or less finely, the slab of caramel.

Use

Use this caramel to sprinkle on your frozen desserts, gelati, creations, et al.

CHOCOLATE SAUCES

Chocolate sauce, hot or cold, is a choice side dish for gelati and frozen desserts. Always choose a quality chocolate, containing at least 65 percent cacao.

Difficulty: easy
Serves: 4 to 6 people
Preparation time: 10 minutes
Cooking time: 1 minute

INGREDIENTS:
Chocolate sauce served hot:
1¼ cup whole milk
1 Tbsp powdered bitter cocoa
⅛ cup cornstarch
10 oz dark chocolate (at least 65 percent cacao), grated or chopped

Milk chocolate sauce served rather cold:
1 cup milk
½ vanilla bean
2 oz grated milk chocolate
1 oz grated dark chocolate
⅛ cup powdered sugar
2 egg yolks
1 level tsp cornstarch

The sauces presented here are rather different. The first one is very dense with powerful and direct aromas. The second is sweeter, milkier, and, somehow, more sensual.

CHOCOLATE SAUCE SERVED HOT

Beat the cold milk with the cocoa and cornstarch. Let it simmer in a saucepan on medium, while whisking, then remove the saucepan immediately from the heat. Add the chopped chocolate and combine until it melts completely. Serve hot, but don't let it boil.

MILK CHOCOLATE SAUCE SERVED RATHER COLD

1. Bring to a simmer the milk and the vanilla bean bent in two lengthwise. Add the chocolates.

2. In a mixing bowl, whip the sugar and the egg yolks for a moment. Add the cornstarch. Pour the chocolate milk on top, combine, and put it all back in the saucepan. Thicken like a custard, combining, then remove the saucepan from the heat. Take out the vanilla bean. Strain the sauce, let cool.

Use

Arrange the marriages and coupling according to your preferences; there are no rules except for those . . . of good taste! Here are a few alliances that have worked:
• Passion fruit sorbet (p. 92) served with a tiny bowl of very hot chocolate sauce. The contrast of temperatures and flavors is jarring.
• Coffee gelato (p. 92) delicately enhanced by a hint of cold chocolate sauce: a safe bet.
• Bourbon vanilla gelato (p. 66) and hot sauce, a must-eat.
• Fig mascarpone gelato (p. 44) with hot or cold sauce: with a few additional fresh figs sautéed on the stove, delicious!

Tip

If you want to spice up your sauces even a little more, add ⅒ to ⅛ cup of powdered bitter cocoa.

CARAMEL SAUCE

This is the richest sauce—a must-eat no one can resist. One of the keys to its success: the crème fraîche you choose. It should be organic, if possible.

Difficulty: easy
Serves: 4 to 6 people
Preparation time: 10 minutes
Cooking time: 4 to 5 minutes

SPECIAL EQUIPMENT:
parchment paper

INGREDIENTS:
1¾ cups powdered sugar
¼ cup water
1 tbsp glucose powder (p. 26)
1½ cups thick crème fraîche

1. In a saucepan, add the sugar, water, and glucose powder. Combine, then bring to a boil. Boil the resulting syrup on medium-low, never on high. When the sugar begins to brown, place on low heat.

2. Soak a small piece of parchment paper in the forming caramel, then look at it: when the color is pleasantly amber, remove the saucepan from the heat and soak it in a little cold water. Be careful not to burn yourself.

3. Add the crème fraîche (watch out for the steam) heated in a small saucepan. Combine well, then let it cool. Use right away or keep in a hermetically sealed bowl, in the fridge, for 4 or 5 days.

Quick tip
Thus prepared, caramel sauce is rather spiced up and very flavorful. If you want to discover a milkier and sweeter version of it, add ⅓ cup of crème fraîche or light cream.

Tips
You should serve this caramel sauce with gelato and frozen desserts, more than with sorbets, with the notable exception of pear sorbet (p. 102). Marry this sauce with caramel gelato with salted butter (p. 50), panna cotta (p. 184), fior di latte gelato (p. 68), or triflavored frozen bombe (p. 136). As you will note, it's also delicious plain.

COFFEE SAUCE

Coffee sauce must always be used with discretion, since its flavor, rather pronounced, doesn't pair well with all gelati. Prepare it with a freshly ground and fruity mocha.

Difficulty: easy
Serves: about 6 people
Preparation time: 30 minutes
Cooking time: 10 minutes
Setting time: 30 minutes

INGREDIENTS:
2 cups milk
1 tbsp ground mocha
¼ cup light cream
3 egg yolks
⅓ cup powdered sugar
1 Tbsp cornstarch

1. In a saucepan, add the milk, coffee, and cream, then give it a whisk. Heat, then bring the milk to a simmer. Cover the saucepan, remove it from the heat, let infuse for 30 minutes, then strain with a very fine strainer.

2. At this point, combine the egg yolks and the sugar in a mixing bowl with a whisk. Add the cornstarch, combine. Pour the coffee milk on top. Combine thoroughly. Pour this preparation in the saucepan and heat on low, stirring continually for about 7 to 8 minutes. When the sauce thickens (at a temperature of 185°F, if you have a thermometer), remove the saucepan from the heat. Immediately filter the sauce through a fine strainer, let cool completely. Pour the sauce in a hermetically sealed container and place it without delay in the fridge until ready for use. Don't keep it for more than 2 days.

For a little variety
Coffee sauce pairs well with chocolate, coffee, or cream gelati. Also consider combining it with vanilla and caramel gelati to create beautiful marbled effects on your plates.

CANDIED ORANGE SAUCE

Orange sauce will bring freshness and tartness to your creations. Easy to prepare, it will keep fresh for several days. You can also prepare it with blood orange, tangerine, and even lemon or grapefruit zests.

Difficulty: easy
Serves: about 6 people
Preparation time: 30 minutes
Cooking time: 7 to 8 minutes
Soaking time: 24 hours

SPECIAL EQUIPMENT:
mixer

INGREDIENTS:
Zests:
zest of organic orange (without the white skin)
1½ cups powdered sugar
2 cups water
Sauce:
16 oz cooked white peaches (p. 34)
juice of 1 orange
juice of ½ lemon

1. ZESTS: bring the zests to a boil for a few seconds in a small saucepan with water. Drain them. In a saucepan, add the sugar, water, and blanched whole orange zests. Bring to a boil, let cool. Let soak for 24 hours.

2. SAUCE: briefly drain the peaches, reserving the liquid (you can also use fruits in syrup from the store). In a mixer, add the peaches, ¼ cup of the cooking syrup from the peaches, 3 tablespoons of the cooking syrup from the zests, the orange juice, and the lemon juice. Mix finely, add the drained and finely chopped zests. Taste, add a bit more orange juice or mineral water if the sauce is too thick. Keep in a hermetically sealed container, in the fridge, for 4 or 5 days, but no longer.

Use
Save this sauce for sorbets, serve it in plates and cups, without mixing them up, with strawberry or mango coulis (p. 210). Use it to top dessert shells, for instance (p. 182).

ZABAGLIONE

Plain or flavored, zabaglione is a unique and little-known side dish. Its texture, at once rich and aerated, is unique in its genre.

Difficulty: intermediate
Serves: 4 to 6 people
Preparation time: 30 minutes
Cooking time: 7 to 8 minutes

SPECIAL EQUIPMENT:
electric beater
candy thermometer

INGREDIENTS:
6 egg yolks
1 cup powdered sugar
3 tbsp cold water

1. Beat the egg yolks at medium so that they blanch and, little by little, swell, like stiff whites.

2. At this point, add the sugar and water in a saucepan. Bring to a boil. When the syrup reaches a temperature of 225 to 230°F, remove the saucepan from the heat and pour the hot syrup on the well-beaten yolks (and, above all, beating them continually!). Set the beater on its highest setting, then let cool like that for 5 minutes. Continue to cool, now beating the zabaglione at medium/low for 5 more minutes. At this stage, the zabaglione is ready: use it in the 15 minutes following its production.

For a little variety
With a tablespoon, lay warm on gelati: coconut (p. 70), mascarpone and fig (p. 44), fior di latte (p. 68), bourbon vanilla (p. 66), or cream (p. 54).
Flavor the zabaglione with alcohol: Amaretto, fruit liqueurs, almond-flavored liqueurs, cognac, or Armagnac. You can also add to it (in the yolks, at the beginning of the recipe) the contents of 2 nice vanilla beans, some candied citrus zests, a bit of cinnamon, a hint of cocoa, etc.

APPENDICES

- Glossary, table of recipes, product index . . . -

Amorino, passion and demands...

The Amorino establishment, born in 2002 from the passion of its two creators, Cristiano Sereni and Paolo Benassi, is unalterably faithful to its essential values: demand quality; cultivate steadfastness, pleasure, and taste; and produce flavors and ambiance.

Thanks to this philosophy, success is not delayed and pushes Amorino to set itself up in prestigious addresses like Milan, Berlin, Madrid, London, New York, Lisbon, and more . . . with a goal simply expressed by Paolo Benassi: "to make excellent gelati as naturally as possible, reducing the list of ingredients as much as possible." The effect is immediate: from now on, the throngs in front of Amorino stores are part of the summer scenes. "My greatest satisfaction is to have people discover, through Amorino, the magic of artisanal Italian gelati . . . a part of my native land, my little home," Cristiano Sereni loves to say.

The flavor of a gelato, above all, depends on the attentive choice of each ingredient, but also on the patient and qualitative labor that goes into its preparation. Amorino possesses an acute consciousness of this demanding process. Each new recipe pushes the research of flavors and the pleasure of eating a little further. How? By simply showcasing the organic and the natural, piercing the secret of the origins of each product, but also verifying on the spot the production methods. To have complete mastery of the product and to be able to guarantee excellence to all its clients, such is the credo of Amorino.

Gelati and sorbets are churned daily with respect for the Italian tradition, under the supervision of the head chefs of the establishment. The recipes are accompanied by a chill time that allows the refinement of each aroma and gives the time for each flavor to affirm its very character. Only free-range organic eggs and high-quality whole milk as the foundation of the gelato. Neither artificial aroma nor artificial coloring has a place in Amorino gelati: such is the fundamental tenet of the company's work.

GLOSSARY

Amaretti
Traditional Italian recipe of little almond cookies, like macaroons.

Bones of the Dead
Traditional Venetian cookies made with flour, butter, and sugar.

Brown sugar
Brown-colored sugar obtained by the crystallization of cane sugar, as opposed to white powdered sugar, which comes from beets.

Brown sugar (Demarara)
Type of caramel-colored, unrefined cane sugar. A product of Reunion Island.

Brown sugar (Muscovado)
Type of unrefined cane sugar with a taste of spices and licorice. A product of Mauritius Island.

Cantucci (Biscotti)
Rustic cookies made with a bread dough enriched with oil and anise seeds.

Chilling
Resting time necessary for a preparation before reusing in order to finish making a recipe.

Contents
Culinary term that refers to the all the products (flour, butter, eggs . . .) needed for the creation of a preparation during the process of making it.

Double boiler
Cooking method allowing you to cook gradually or to melt an ingredient, which consists of putting the container with the ingredients in another larger container of hot water.

Lining
Culinary technique that helps facilitate removal from a mold. It consists of lining the sides of a mold with butter, then flour, parchment paper, caramel . . .

Skimming
Culinary technique that consists of removing, with the help of a skimmer or another utensil, the foam that forms on the surface of a liquid when cooking.

TABLE OF RECIPES

Mont Blanc cup	168	Pear cup and chocolate, "homemade" baked wafers	194
Napoleon (frozen, with hazelnuts, meringue, vanilla, and red berries)	148	Sauce (candied orange)	220
Napoleon (strawberry, lemon, and passion fruit)	172	Sauce (caramel)	216
		Sauce (coffee)	218
Oranges and lemons (frosted)	146	Sauce (vanilla)	202
Panettone (Chantilly cream, caramelized pistachios)	192	Sauces (chocolate)	214
		Semifreddo (bourbon vanilla)	180
Panna cotta, panna cotta gelato, caramel, fruits	184	Smoothie (Alphonso mango)	124
		Smoothie (coffee)	120
Parfait (frozen bourbon vanilla)	142	Smoothie (raspberry)	122

PRODUCT INDEX

ACKNOWLEDGMENTS

*The editor (Éditions du Chêne) would like to thank Cristiano Sereni
for his confidence, Laura Casini for her support and her concern,
and Stéphanie Claux for her responsiveness and her efficiency.*

*At the same time, she would like to thank Thomas Dhellemmes
and Cécile Coulier, as well as all the members of the
l'Atelier May 98 team (Nicolas, Jérémie, Caroline . . .),
for their dynamism and their creativity.*

*It would also like to thank Stéphan Lagorce for his ear,
his patience, and his availability.*

*Amorino would like to thank Laura, without whom the Amorino angel
would not exist. Let us thank her, as well, for her passion for cooking
that she has put to the service of the making of this work.*

Amorino would also like to thank Stéphan Lagorce for his ear.

*At the same time, Amorino would like to thank
Franco Stagni and Romuald Herbaux for their help.*

*Amorino would like to thank the photo production team,
Thomas Dhellemmes and Cécile Coulier.*

*Finally, and of course, Éditions du Chêne
and in particular Juliette de Lavaur,
who launched the company into this adventure . . .*

CREDITS

MANAGING EDITOR
Juliette de Laveur

EDITORIAL ASSISTANT
Françoise Mathay,
assisted by Marion Dellapina

ART DIRECTION
Sabine Houplain,
assisted by Claire Mieyeville
and Audrey Lorel

GRAPHIC DESIGN
Ximena Riveros

GRAPHIC PRODUCTION
Aurore Jannin

PROOFREADING
Isabelle Macé

PRODUCTION
Nicole Thiériot-Pichon

PHOTOENGRAVING
Quat'coul